Adult ADHD: What You Need to Know

David Gurevich

Copyright © 2010 David Gurevich

All rights reserved.

ISBN: 1456424521
ISBN-13: 978-1456424527

DEDICATION

Dedicated to my family, to Professor Barrett Hazeltine, and Nancy. Thanks for all the support and being there!

CONTENTS

Dedication	i
Introduction	Pg 1
Adult ADHD Test	Pg 4
I Think I Might Have ADHD!	Pg 18
Why is ADHD Ignored in Adults?	Pg 24
Common Questions About ADHD	Pg 33
ADHD Medications - The Basics	Pg 54
10 Ways to Prove ADHD Exists	Pg 78
The 4 Secrets to Success with ADHD	Pg 88
Dr. Tuckman Answers Q's on Adult ADHD	Pg 93
Your Career and ADHD	Pg 107
10 Most Important ADHD Meds	Pg 115
25 Life Tips	Pg 133

1. INTRODUCTION

How many adults in the United States have ADHD, or attention deficit hyperactivity disorder?

If you were like most psychiatrists and doctors in the year 1990, you'd have answered, "almost none. The condition is typically characterized by hyperactivity, which most adults don't have. And even without hyperactivity, just ADD, there simply isn't that much of it in adults."

They were horribly wrong. According to the World Health Organization and many other respected medical authorities, about 5% of adults in the United States have ADHD.[1]

That's 11,000,000 people.

Because we didn't believe ADHD existed in adults, not very many are getting treatment. Of those eleven million, in the past year, only one million got some form of treatment for ADHD.

This is a gigantic public health failure. Untreated ADHD causes real problems. Having it means you're twice as likely to get a divorce. You have an up to 50% chance of developing serious depression or anxiety.[2] You're more likely to get your license suspended or revoked.[3]

All this – and you would have had no idea why.

Why it was so hard for you to pay attention to small details, to sit still, to stay focused on one thing. To enjoy a long conversation or stay at the dinner table after eating. Those and more than 90 other areas can be extremely challenging for people with ADHD.[3]

The worst part? We now can show almost conclusively that ADHD is a physical condition. The evidence is extremely strong and only growing. We can now, for instance, measure your brain waves and tell you with about 90% accuracy if you have ADHD or not.[4]

By the time you finish reading this guide, you will know what adult ADHD looks like, what to do if you think you might have it, and a good deal about how it is treated.

This is a no-nonsense booklet. It was written to be as short as possible while being scientifically accurate and providing comprehensive information. You can print it and read it while taking the bus to work, for instance.

2. ADULT ADHD TEST

Here are 33 ways that ADHD can manifest in someone's life. As you read each one, mentally note if, "yes, that's me." If you think "yes" more than a few times, then you may have ADHD.

Please note that this is a somewhat informal test.

1) **You sit down to study** something you don't want to. Five minutes later, you've decided that it isn't worth doing, that it's not important, that you're not interested in it – whatever.

You come up with a reason so you don't have to study.

2) Someone can be talking directly to you, but you get either really irritated – you want to talk about something else – or start to zone out and not really hear what they're saying.

3) **Is something boring?** If something is boring, then doing it feels like your mind was put into a blender and then sucked through a straw.[17]

If something is interesting, however, you can do it for hours without getting tired or losing interest.

4) You tend to **get lost while driving**. Additionally, you tend to lose your anger or get frustrated with the other people on the road. Why do they drive so fast? Or so close to your car?

5) You are **really excited** about a new idea until someone **points out a flaw** in it. Then you lose enthusiasm like a deflated balloon. Many of your great ideas die when they turn out to take more work than expected.

6) Over the course of a day, you may go from **one extreme** mood **to another**. You may feel like things are great, lose excitement, get bored, get excited and so on – all in the course of a day.

7) You can **watch television**, talk on **instant message**, and **do crossword puzzles** – all at the same time. You actually find it relaxing, or that you focus better.

8) People can sit at the dinner table and talk for hours. Say it's just a plain old dinner and not on one of your favorite topics **do you leave the dinner** as fast as possible?

9) Are there periods where you get really excited about something and just slip into a zone where that is all you think about? Hours go by like seconds.

It's called hyperfocus, and if that name "clicks" with you, than it's likely you have it.

10) **You're playing video games** or doing something fun, when someone you know starts talking to you. "Why don't you take out the garbage, please?"

"I said I'll do it – after I finish doing what I'm doing. Why don't you trust me?"

"Because I need it right now. Please! You're not even doing anything right now!"

A fight ensues.

Sound familiar?

11) You're in math class. The teacher is talking: "So if you add 3 + 4 and.."

"it's 7!" you call out.

The teacher coughs, gives you a black look, and goes on -"So if you add 3 + 4 and multiply by 2..."

12) Sometimes you can just **zone out**. Time flies by, you're deeply relaxed and thinking about things that have absolutely nothing to do with what or where you are – like life in general.

13) **You're in Paris** with some friends, and deciding what to do. "Okay, first we'll see the Louvre, then hit the National Museum, then see a juggling show, then..."

Sound like you? When you're in the groove, you're a powerhouse of energy.

14) Sometimes you **get really angry** for no reason, or shout at someone for stupid reasons. The anger doesn't make that much sense and it goes away really quickly too.

15) **You're supposed to do something**, but you forgot or lost the things you need to do it.

16) You notice things all over the room that are extremely random or irrelevant.

Like, for instance, in a meeting, you may notice the clicking of pens, the leaves falling outside, and so on – all while you should be paying attention.

17) You are wondering if you could be doing something more interesting than reading this list.

18) **When you start getting bored**, you have to move physically or do something different. Now! And if you sit still

for too long, you almost feel physical pain in your head. It's hard to describe.

19) **Hitchhiking** through the amazons while writing a book and making new friends with the natives – does that sound like an ideal trip?

20) **You're at the coffee shop** with a friend, and you're ordering. "That'll be a triple shot espresso, please!"

Your friend looks at you. "How are you going to fall asleep? And…umm, aren't you a little hyper already?"

You smile. "It actually makes me think better." (Friend in the back of her mind mumbles, *It makes everyone think better…*)

You down the coffee and feel calmer. Then you have an hour long conversation about the new dynamics at work, take a walk and really connect.

21) **You are the first** to start new things, like wearing multicolored socks. When things start to become cool, you can be among those who make it so – adopting them before everyone else.

You might find yourself ahead of trends because you're always looking for something new.

22) When you love someone, you think nothing of spending hours on them, noticing what's really important to them, and being very romantic.

Your ability to focus can make you an irresistible charmer – when you're interested.

23) "We're going to have to start using this new program." One week later, you've pretty much figured everything about it, while everyone else is complaining about the change.

When you have to update all your files to the new format, however, you don't get round to doing it for a long, long time.

24) You're always interested in making new friends. Frankly, they're usually more interesting than your old friends!

25) Since you've **gotten lost** so many times, as long as nothing important is happening, you just enjoy getting to see something new. It sometimes is fun.

26) You can be very loyal, sticking with someone when everyone else abandons them

27) When **you find something interesting**, you can learn everything about it.

When someone tells you something about it, you don't forget it, either. For that one thing, you are a supergenius.

28) **You just finished** a lecture and you are the first to start clapping. Are you among the first to react to things?

29) Someone walks up behind you, **shouts "boo!"** You hardly flinch. You just have a feel for what's going on in a room, and aren't easily caught off guard.

30) Do you quickly forget what happened or the past, or not feel like it's important? Are you always doing something new?

31) **Your new boss wants** to try a marketing method you feel is highly immoral.

Everyone else in the office tells you to wait, that the approval process for sure will make it cleaner and more appropriate But you feel you have to do something right away.

When you next bump into your new boss, you blurt out how you feel.

32) **You're in a meeting** when you can't wait anymore. You blurt out, "But why don't we try doing this? Am I the only one who noticed we don't have a real marketing plan?"

Sometimes you seem to notice things others don't. That said, sometimes you might say something impulsively that everyone kind of laughs at.

It can be embarrassing. Because even if you have a good point, if not delivered the right way, it can be taken the wrong way.

33) When you want to get something done, you get it done. The way you get there might be totally bizarre, strange, exotic – whatever. But you get there.

3. OKAY, TELL ME MORE

ADHD is a fairly common condition. Around 5% of adults have it. It is a condition characterized by differences in attention, energy and impulse control.

An exact diagnosis is done by a trained specialist who analyses your performance on certain tests, gives you a thorough work-up, and knows what to look for.

If you have trouble focusing on things, paying attention to small details, a constant need to be doing something new, or simply can't sit still for too long – then you should seriously consider if ADHD might be an issue.

Reading on will expose you to some questions that focus more on problem areas.

We'll also go into why the DSM IV is highly flawed as a diagnostic tool for adult ADHD.

Some questions to ask yourself

Some questions you may consider are: do you have trouble doing things that require sustained mental effort for a long period of time?

The key is *not* if you can do things that you enjoy for long periods of time. Rather, can you spend prolonged periods of attention on things that don't interest you but have to be done?

Manifestations of this can be a strange feeling of anxiety and restlessness. You might be able to sit and study for 10 minutes, but then need to get up and pace. *Most people don't have that problem.*

Do you have trouble doing things in order? One study had no one without ADHD have that problem, while almost 50% of those with it did.[3]

In general, do you often get lost, have difficulty following extended instructions? Are you very impatient, or do you have trouble paying attention to things? If someone talks directly to you, do you have difficulty listening or paying attention?

Are you an aggressive driver? Do you frequently lose patience on the road? Difficulties with driving are a strong indicator of ADHD, and have been proposed by some as part of a diagnostic appraisal for adults.

Can you play video games for hours? Being able to get lost and spend hours in a video game while not doing the work that needs to be done is a classic ADHD behavior.

Socially: are your friendships short, overly intense, or have unpleasant endings? Do you have difficulty developing long term relationships? Do you have difficulty staying with someone once you find them boring?

Professionally: are you not progressing as expected? Do you often get told your work is not up to par? Or do you start projects with a great deal of energy, then run out of steam?

Educationally: do you have trouble sitting down and studying – despite being very motivated or strongly wanting to do so?

Is your performance at school significantly lower than it should be considering your intelligence? Do you have trouble reading things from start to finish?

I can't have it. I'm not hyperactive.

Not true. Actually, in adults, we're starting to know more and more that hyperactivity is different. You may feel over energetic or restless, but not actually have hyperactivity.[6]

And even if you don't have problems with too much energy, you can still have ADD.

But I'm successful.

Being successful does *not* mean you don't have ADHD. It just means that you have developed positive ways of dealing with it.

Some of the most successful people I know have ADHD – but with treatment, are finally able to deal with the issues that had been holding them back, perhaps without them even noticing.

But I can spend a lot of time doing things I enjoy.

The ability to pay attention to enjoyable things also does not mean you don't have ADHD. On the contrast, you may spend hours doing things you enjoy – while not filing your taxes, finishing that report, or taking care of some other boring chores.

4. THE DSM IV AND ADULT ADHD

Using the DSM IV, which is the standard diagnostic manual, for ADHD in people over 16 is a travesty because the test for ADHD is entirely focused on children.[3] Someone who has ADHD, for instance, it says, may do the following: "often runs or climbs excessively" in situations that are inappropriate.[5]

Take a medical student with ADHD and has been having trouble staying on top of things. He probably does not have a climbing on things inappropriately problem.

Yes, the test does add a parenthesis: "(in adolescents or adults, may be limited to subjective feelings of restlessness)"

The parenthesis is there because the diagnostic test is showing that it is first and foremost treating ADHD as something kids have, and possibly adolescents or adults.

Further proof?

The first paragraph says, that to have ADHD, you have to have symptoms in a way that "is maladaptive and inconsistent with developmental level."

The DSM considers ADHD a developmental disorder – the fundamental idea is that ADHD means that you're not as developed as your peers, but don't worry. You'll catch up with them, and until then you can take Ritalin.

This ignores the fact that ADHD is often a chronic lifelong condition. Additionally, what is an appropriate developmental level for someone who is 35?

There are other significant problems with the current conception of ADHD in adults. The main key is that hyperactivity may not be present to the same degree. A kid may have tons of physical energy, but an adult with ADHD may have other symptoms.

We need a test for adult ADHD that is based off the problems they have. Researcher Barkley and his colleagues have come up with a list of just 9 questions that is extremely accurate at diagnosing ADHD[3] which should be a strong contender for inclusion in the DSM V.

The curious are recommended to obtain a copy of his work, Adult ADHD: What the Science Says.

5. I THINK I MIGHT HAVE ADHD!

So you read the 33 snapshots, saw yourself in them, and then read a little more about what the symptoms of ADHD are. You really are starting to feel – or already felt – that you have it. Now what?

The first step is patience. As hard as it may be, you need to thoroughly examine all the factors and come up with a plan that makes sense. Get more information!

Read on in this book to learn more about what ADHD looks like, what treatment entails, and some general ideas on how to succeed despite it. Check out the recommended books.

Join some online forums, see what other people are going through.

But, okay, you've done that. And you still think you have ADHD. Before you go on, the first question you want to ask yourself is, *Does this really impact my life?*

Be honest. You could forget your keys every day, have way too much energy, and extremely impulsive – you might just be a Hollywood celebrity.

Jokes aside, you want to get a really good understanding of if there are problems in your life that are being caused by ADHD. It's only when something is not going right that treatment is called for.

Remember, *You can not diagnose yourself.* Only a doctor can make the official diagnosis of ADHD.

Even if you have all the symptoms of ADHD, you may not have it. There are many conditions that cause similar symptoms and that may require treating themselves. Being hyperactive may be caused by hyperthyroidism, for instance, and poor attention span can come with depression.

Remember, 95% of people *don't* have ADHD.

How do I find a doctor?

This is a tricky area. We could provide you with a list of the best doctors in the 50 US States, but that wouldn't work – they're the best for a reason, and waiting for an appointment could take a while. Plus it would let down readers from, say, East Africa.

One solid way to find a doctor is by referral. Your primary care physician probably knows some excellent psychiatrists.

Or you can go to someone you know whom you trust, say a family friend who is a doctor, and ask them for a referral. You can be subtle – say you're asking on behalf of a very close friend. Even if you do tell them your concerns, part of being a doctor is having tight lips.

You could try asking a clergyman at Church, a Rabbi at synagogue or an Imam at Mosque. They have to know about such things – modern life is too difficult, and more people than you might think choose to get help. Another place to try is your local health center.

Make sure that you get someone who has experience with adult ADHD.

What happens at the doctor?

Your doctor will evaluate how things are going in your life and decide how to proceed. It is not unheard of for someone to see a doctor for the first time and leave with a prescription for an ADHD medication.

Considering the high street value, however, of the medications, as well as their potential for side effects and abuse, it is also quite typical to undergo a more extensive evaluation.

How much evaluation you get can vary. You may be asked to perform a variety of tests from which the doctor will try to understand how you operate.

If a diagnosis of ADHD is reached upon, most likely your doctor will recommend treatment with a medication, and you'll have to decide whether or not you want to do so.

To help you, we'll go into the exact medication options, what they do, and what it's like to be on a stimulant medication later on in this book.

If you decide not to take medication, then treatment will focus on helping you understand how you experience things differently from most people.

Importantly, it will help you find ways to reach better outcomes. Instead of trying to change what you can't, therapy would help you find ways to accomplish things using your strengths and finding solutions to your weaknesses.

Even with medication, getting some therapy is a good idea. The effects of ADHD medications are, at the right dose, subtle. You need the help of a therapist to understand how to use your improved attention span in a constructive manner, and guidance to adjusting to a new way of living.

Otherwise, for instance, you may take your Ritalin, but because you're still not organized, forget to finish your report just as though you hadn't taken anything.

The ultimate goal of therapy is to improve the quality of your life. And for treatment of ADHD, the goal is to reduce the impact that not paying attention, hyperactivity and impulsivity have on your life.

Getting where you want to be may take a while, but with time, you should find yourself needing to meet with your therapist less and less often. While you may value the relationship you develop with her, this is a healthy process – ideally, you should be fine by yourself.

6. THE 10 REASONS ADULT ADHD IS IGNORED

1) Until 2000, we didn't really believe adults had ADHD. It turns out that as people get older, they typically become less hyperactive.

Since this is the key symptom that people use to diagnose ADHD – attention deficit **hyperactivity** disorder – we used to believe adults didn't have it.

But it turns out they do. Around 5% of adults have ADHD, but most don't have physical hyperactivity, but rather a sense of restlessness or need to always be doing something new/exciting. They have ADD, or attention deficit disorder.

2)   We used to believe that adults outgrew ADHD. Again, this was because the typical hyperactivity symptom diminishes with age. It turns out that up to 50% of kids who have ADHD will also have it in some significant form as an adult.

Importantly, people think they stop being ADHD. If asked at age 20, a very significant amount of people who had ADHD as kids will say they no longer have it. When asked again at age 27, many of those realize that they still have it, and only thought it was gone.[3]

3)   Doctors don't know how to diagnose adult ADD/ADHD. In one study of 400 primary care physicians, they referred patients to a specialist for depression only 2% of the time. So 98% of the time, they were confident in diagnosing depression.

In contrast, half didn't feel confident in diagnosing adult ADHD, and 66% of the time the doctor referred people who they thought had it to specialists.[1]

Now, this isn't to say that a primary care physicians role is that of psychiatrist. Society, unfortunately, due to economic and social constraints, has them play that role for many sociological conditions.

So they are doing so, and are comfortable diagnosing ADHD in a kid, when, arguably, there is a lot more at risk. They aren't comfortable diagnosing adult ADHD because there still aren't clear guidelines for doing so.

The DSM, which is "the book" in diagnosing psychiatric conditions, is written for kids. The diagnostic criteria simply do not work in adults for multiple reasons, as discussed earlier in this booklet.

4) Adults with ADHD don't get help. Only around 10% of adults with ADD/ADHD received treatment in the past year. This is important because up to half of people with ADHD also experience depression and/or serious anxiety issues.

Because treatment works fairly well, quickly and can be life-changing for those who get it – and those who live, work and spend time with them - this is a serious public health issue.

5) A lot of people believe, *If someone is successful, they can't have ADHD.* Or, *if someone is at Harvard they obviously don't have ADHD.* This simply isn't true. Adults can learn compensating behaviors that shield their symptoms. For their chronic disorganization, for instance, they may rely on an assistant or their spouse.

In fact, when able to control the negative aspects, people with ADHD can be extremely successful. They make great entrepreneurs, artists and visionaries because they don't focus on the small details but rather what excites them – the big picture, helping people, drawing an amazing picture.

6) We don't have a good "testing ground" for ADHD in adults.[7] For kids, everyone has to sit through many years of school, which requires extended concentration in stuff that, frankly, isn't always interesting. This environment is perfect for making people with ADHD struggle. Their problems cause noticeable issues, so they get help.

Adults, however, don't have that. If a job is getting boring or takes too much concentration, you can always switch. And you don't have parents to judge or force you to take a socially accepted road.

This means that, rather than deal with the underlying ADHD problem, adults with it might just find compensating behaviors that may or may not be helpful to some degree (switching jobs, probably not so good. Having an assistant, probably good – for anyone!)

7) The symptoms of ADHD can be very subtle.[7] People with prominently inattentive symptoms may simply just seem too much of a pushover or eager to please. Someone with ADHD might be doing just fine at their job, but never get round to passing a certification test for a promotion.

A key thing to look at is, *is someone performing significantly worse than they should for no reason?* For instance, has an adult with an IQ of 143 been stuck for several years at an entry level position? (Or does a student with great smarts and desire to do well get C's and D's in college?)

8) ADHD seems to go away sometimes. When you have one day to finish a proposal, you might seem like you have incredible focus. When you're selling to a new prospect, you might be able to talk and listen *perfectly* – as if all your concentration is fully engaged with understanding them by relating to them so you can sell.

When you are under a lot of pressure, highly caffeinated, or simply really enjoy something, it probably doesn't seem like you have any attention issues at all.

Unfortunately, most of life is relaxed and not high pressure, and it is in non "do-or-die" situations that your problem emerges.

9) Denial and over confidence.

Some people exhibit the negative lifestyle outcomes of ADHD (underperformance, mild to serious depression, anxiety at performing extended periods of concentration, too many friendships/relationships, inability to settle down, follow a directed path – and so on) but don't believe they might have it.

They may feel that in general they are doing too well to have that disorder, or that ADHD is a savvy creation of marketing wizards. (Now, their skepticism is for very good reason. Drug companies do spend a significant amount of money on marketing conditions to indirectly sell their drugs, and we simply must not ignore the influence they have on how we think about health and conditions.)

Making it harder, people with ADHD are, like most people, but perhaps a little more so, inclined to be overconfident. This may in part be caused by a short memory, high energy level, and strong resilience.

Unfortunately, they may be firm in their belief that they don't have issues to deal with – even as they go through friendships, relationships and jobs at a quick rate, or suffer from anxiety, depression or other problems.

They might, for instance, if you forced them to take an ADHD self-diagnostic test (and got truthful answers!), respond positive to many of the symptoms – but then quickly argue that it's just normal. As we will discuss, yes, the symptoms of ADHD are arguably all normal – but not when they're present as a cluster, persistent, chronic, and present significant life problems.

Additionally, trying to talk about a difficult subject with someone with ADHD can backfire. They might throw the idea out offhand, not even thinking about it.

10) In sum: People don't know what ADHD in adults look like. If you happen to worry about the problems in your life, you may hit the web and look up the symptoms. "ADHD" – needs to have, XYX. "Well, I'm not that hyper, really."

Or you may justifiably be concerned that the condition is based off normal human experiences. If you discuss your concerns with their primary doctor, he is much more likely than not to *not* realize what it is. And people aren't always very ADD in the doctors office!

If you see a shrink, and they don't realize it's ADHD, treatment may have little to no benefit. Your sessions may consist of conversations about irrelevant topics, or you simply might not think of anything to say.

And you might get mood stabilizers because you may seem like you have bipolar disorder (with your mood and energy fluctuations) or antidepressants.

Antidepressants are not a bad idea – when depression is a serious problem in and of itself. People with ADHD, however, tend to be depressed because of the failures and challenges in their lives. For many, to be happy they have to change those outcomes for the better.

The end result? Many years of frustration and way too many unexplained failures ("What happened to that project you were working on?" Excited look. "Oh, I started something much more interesting!") You may get stuck in a life pattern that is simply not fun, enjoyable or productive.

7. COMMON QUESTIONS ABOUT ADHD

Why is it called Attention Deficit Hyperactivity Disorder?

People with ADHD have attention deficits when made to do something they don't want to. And they can sometimes seem to have too much energy, to be hyperactive. So they don't really pay attention to what they should be doing, but have tons of energy to do other things.

Of course, in adults, there may be less hyperactivity. In that case, it could just be plain attention deficit disorder, no 'H.' (But for simplification, this book uses ADHD to include both).

That doesn't sound exactly right...?

Yes, it doesn't. People with ADHD don't really have a deficit of attention. I'm fairly sure this isn't an original thought because it's so obvious, but it seems more and more that ADD/ADHD should be called "attention *dysregulation* disorder."

The problem isn't not being able to focus. A person with ADHD might be able to spend hours reading, playing video games, or chatting to several people online.

The challenge? Being able to focus in situations that aren't enjoyable or high stimulus.

An emergency room surgeon with ADHD might seem extremely capable of focusing as she extracts a bullet from a kid.[8]

A business executive with ADHD might seem incredibly savvy when he orders the company to change to a new technology. And an artist might seem to have great focus when she spends several days straight working on a new piece – while ignoring the bills piling up in the mail.

Are people with ADHD similar?

People with ADHD tend to be very, very different from one another. That's because the condition, which has a common underlying cause, has as an end result something that is very personal – if you are interested in something, you can do it, and otherwise may find it extremely hard.

As such, the condition of ADHD can be found in a very wide variety of people – from celebrities and dancers, to mathematicians and plumbers.

Why does ADHD exist?

Something like ADHD must exist for a reason – something so common yet disruptive couldn't be that common if it didn't have some sort of benefit. For instance, the mutation of sickle cell anemia, where blood cells are misshapen, leads to significant health problems. But it also protects people from malaria, which is why it is fairly common in Africa.

As such, there must be benefits that ADHD has.

What benefit could having ADHD have?

Writer Thom Hartmann came up with a metaphor that instantly struck me as accurate, and hopefully will help you too.

It happened when his son came home from school shaken. Concerned, his Dad, Thom, asked him what was going on. They thought he had attention deficit/hyperactivity disorder. Thom was also not so happy – was his son, who he loved beyond words, defective? Deficit, defective, bad – right?

The more Thom thought about it, the more he came to wonder if there wasn't a better way to put things. Maybe having ADHD was like being a hunter versus being a farmer.[8]

Back in the day, when we humans were weak, dispersed, and far from being the rulers of the planet (which we are still not – global warming being just one proof of our inability to manage the environment), there were several ways of getting food.

The oldest way, and this is going to the very beginning, was to hunt. People would get their food from hunting. The people who were best at that? Restless, impatient, always looking for something to chase and kill. Responsive to change. If the animals were moving, then the hunters had to as well. To not be extremely sensitive to the hunting game meant death.

But things changed. People slowly learned different ways of living, and started to realize the benefits of farming. Now that called for an entirely different type of person. To be a farmer, you had to be patient.

You'd sow seeds now and carefully tend them – and you'd have to wait for them to grow. You had to have organizational skills – if you didn't manage your food supply well *then* you'd die.

People who used to be great hunters now had to spend their days doing things that they found, well, boring.

Sadly for those hunter personality types, farming has been the dominant model for at least the last several thousand years, and even more so today.

The proof? To make it in today's society, you have to: a) go to school for 12 years, learning things you have no choice or control over, being tested and judged all the way b) go to college for 4 more years.

Then, in the work place you have to sit through long meetings, submit projects that you work on for several months – and are expected to have made no small little mistakes on.

Not fun for the hunter.

Okay, so that model may or may not work for you. The important thing to realize is that the hunter model is a positive way to capture both the positive and negative aspects of ADHD.

Why do so many people with ADHD have anxiety or depression?

There is a pattern that happens time and time again in people with ADHD. It can make you think you're stupid or incapable, that you're different, that you'll never succeed. It's tragic. And I bet you'll see yourself in it.

The pattern is as follows. You start out with a healthy self-confidence and ego. You are a normal person and there's no reason that you can't do what other people do. If other people can, say, study for a test, you can too. *1) You expect to be able to do something*

Then you try to do whatever it is that you feel you should be able to do. For some weird reason, however, you can't do it right. When you sit down to study, you find out that your notes are unreadable, or that you simply can't sit still.

And because there was a pretty good reason you had to study (prepare, whatever), you end up with a result that really sucks. *2) You fail to do it*

You get a bad grade. You get yelled at. Life isn't fun.

The next time a test comes up you have a quite different attitude. You know you're not going to be able to study for it, so you don't try so hard. Not surprisingly, you don't do well. *3) You anticipate failure*

Now, failure after failure comes. You already believe you can't do something – and that makes 100% sense. Why would you be able to succeed where you've always failed? And the worst part? Everyone else can do it! And no one believes you when you tell them you can't do it!

"Oh, Mark, if you only tried you'd do better in class. You're so smart, why don't you just study?"

"I can't."

They give you a weird look, walk away. You're just lazy to them.

4) You get depressed. You can't do things and are failing in many ways – so it makes sense that you don't believe in yourself.

Yet things look up. You realize that you can start a business selling hand-made armchairs, or you decide that things are going to be different. Of course you can study and make it through college!

And whatever new project you start goes off to a great beginning. Before long, however, you lose your excitement. Reality sets in, and you have yet another failure on your belt.

For instance. Imagine you're a student studying immunology and it's a few days before the test.

"Okay, I have to study for Immunology now," you think. But you feel really nervous about it – you've never been able to study for an extended period of time. Still, you want to do well in the class, and there's nothing wrong with you, right? You can do it!

So the next day you take your textbook, sit down in the library. After ten minutes, you feel this horrible feeling that you really couldn't describe. Basically, you'd rather be doing anything than studying. But it's really important that you do well in class!

With all your might, and the help of a cup of coffee, you get another 15 minutes in. Then you simply can't do anymore, you leave.

You get a D on the test. When talking to a friend as you walk out of class, you mention how upset you were with your grade. She knows you fairly well and just says, "Well, how long did you study?"

Here's what happens

People with ADHD associate a great deal of anxiety with normal activities. This is a learned habit that is caused by repeated failure and painful outcome. When someone with ADHD fails at sitting down and studying, it causes pain and hard associations.

Now, fortunately, one of the benefits that comes with ADHD is a short memory and ability to keep trying. This can sometimes mean, however, that the failures keep happening, and eventually become too much.

Just the thought of doing that activity becomes painful.

In summation, here is the pattern that happens in ADHD and leads to depression and anxiety.

1) You expect to be able to do something. *You're normal, so of course you can pass math class!*

2) You fail to do it. *Other people don't get why you can't do it, so you don't get much support, which only makes it harder.*

3) You anticipate failure, so don't try as hard. *This ensures that you will fail next time.*

4) You get depressed. *You can't do things, other people can – it's not fair. Why bother?*

Those who get treatment for ADHD often spend time figuring out how to break this cycle and have more positive outcomes.

Can diet and environmental factors cause ADHD?

There has been limited research into whether or not diet can cause symptoms of ADHD, and what has done has mostly been negative or mixed.

One study of 100 kids with ADHD showed that many had somewhat increased levels of lead in their blood.[9] A similar study, however, which reduced lead levels via treatment did not show any improvement in symptoms.

Additionally, people with ADHD may have slightly lower blood iron levels than people without.[9] Again, however, treatment to increase iron levels did not improve symptoms.

Other studies looked at whether supplementation with omega-3 fatty acids and other oils would decrease hyperactivity and impulsivity while increasing attention. The results have been mixed.

At best, the studies show slight improvements on some scales (like the Parental Rating of Hyperactivity) while no benefit on other scales, like the Teacher Rating.

Dr. Ben Feingold suggested that consuming synthetic food colors and flavors alongside naturally occurring salicylates may cause hyperactivity.[10]

As a treatment, he suggested a highly restrictive diet, and reported that his diet worked in 50% of cases. Scientific research, however, into his approach has been both lacking and not particularly compelling. It seems to show that the Feingold diet mostly doesn't work except in a very small subset of children in whom it may have a benefit.

One of the more interesting areas, however, is research into whether allergies may cause symptoms of ADHD. Having ADHD is itself associated with an increased rate of asthma, stomach aches and ear infections, possibly due to allergic processes.

Researchers decided to investigate whether removing foods that could potentially be allergic from kids diets would reduce ADHD symptoms.

And it did!

In one study, 62 out of 76 kids had a significant improvement in hyperactivity when their diet was changed to remove allergens.[10] Other small studies investigating the same area have shown similar positive results.

Foods that especially provoke allergies? The study reports 79% of kids had allergies to benzoic and tartrazine additives, 67% to cow's milk, 54% to chocolate and 45% to oranges.[10]

While these studies have not been accepted as scientific norm, they indicate that dietary approaches may hold some worth in treatment of ADHD. Remember, "you are what you eat."

8. COMMON ISSUES WITH ADHD

"ADHD is just a variation of normal behavior"

Yes and no. Yes, most people do experience ADHD symptoms, and anyone could be described as having ADHD if you are loose enough with how you diagnose it. That said, there is a clear difference between the extreme, chronic and not controllable attentional problems people with ADHD have – and the normal mental fatigue that comes with work and focus.

It's partly like this. Someone with ADHD might only be able to spend 5 minutes focusing on something they don't enjoy, or even less. In conversations, people with ADHD might have difficulty staying focused even for several minutes.

By contrast, most people can focus on things even if they aren't fully enjoyable for much greater periods of time.

Remember, according to Dr. Barkley's research, there are at least 91 symptoms where people with ADHD tend to have significantly more trouble than people who don't (and people who don't have ADHD but do have other psychological conditions.)

The fact is that almost *all* psychological conditions could be argued to be variants of normal behavior. Someone with Obsessive Compulsive Disorder could be marginalized as simply being in the 99th percentile for anxiety. Even the conditions like schizophrenia are actually not too far removed from normal existence.

If you were locked in a room by yourself (but given food through a tray so you didn't starve) and left alone for a week, there is a good chance that you would start hallucinating or becoming delusional.

Physical issues like pain also go on a continuum. We absolutely have the duty to treat someone who breaks their leg with as strong painkillers as are needed, even though their pain is nothing more than an extension of what you'd feel when pricked with a pin.

Not only that, we now view it as our moral duty to treat normal pain when it is a significant impairment to quality of life. When a woman gives birth, we don't think about the many thousands of years that it was a completely natural experience. If it is safe and requested, we provide her with painkillers.

What's it like to have ADHD?

What someone with ADHD experiences when he or she tries to focus on something they don't want to is a type of mental pain. Imagine how you would feel if you had just left a 3 hour pitch to convince a skeptical client to buy your product – and then your boss told you to solve a theoretical physics problem, or he'd fire you.

That kind of mental exhaustion, anxiety and panic, is a lot similar to what someone with ADHD might feel when they have to sit down for an hour and study for class.

Having to pay attention in a boring situation is *painful* for someone with ADHD. It's like having a jackhammer drilling on your head, and the worst part is, you know you should be enjoying yourself, being part of the conversation (not dominating it with topics only you find interesting) and so on – but there's nothing you can do.

The jackhammer keeps drilling. You feel anxious because you know you're not getting things the way other people are, but you feel like your mind is suffocating, and you just want to get out of there!

Some describe that trying to pay attention when you're bored and have ADHD is like having the air supply to your brain cut off. Your brain is slowly starving and screaming out for something interesting to happen, getting worse and worse - the more you ignore it the more painful it gets, but the only thing that could help is doing something entirely different.

The worst part? This may happen, say, 5 minutes into an important meeting.

That sounds very interesting, but it's just words. Is there any scientific reason that might happen?

On a neurological level, it seems people with ADHD do *not* have the same signaling pathway that other people do.[11] There is a fundamental difference in how dopamine, a key neurotransmitter, as well as other chemicals are handled. And these chemicals directly determine how we respond to things.

When a normal person does something, their brain rewards them on a moment to moment basis. They can maintain focus and attention because a steady circuit of positive feedback maintains concentration.

Their brains react to the material and send out signals to maintain focus. Research indicates that this pattern may be slower to activate in people with ADHD. Because their brains don't send the maintenance signals as much, maintaining focus becomes extremely difficult.

Imagine trying to lift weights after someone injects a tranquilizer into your arm. If your body does not send the right signals, your muscles simply won't react, and the brain is not too different.

For people with ADHD, to focus there may need to be a very strong, overriding reason (say, a leopard is running at them), or the prospect of immediate reward, which can cause a spike in neural behavior that increases focus.

This is why a lot of people with ADHD are capable of playing video games for hours. The immediate reward loop puts them in a mental state that is focused, excited and very enjoyable.

For them, that circuit almost recreates what normal people experience in day to day life – except playing video games doesn't pay the rent, develop meaningful relationships, or help you pass classes.

But Jack said he has ADHD and he sat perfectly still at a funeral?

A former teacher of mine said he didn't believe in ADHD because people who had it seemed to have no trouble sitting still at, say, a funeral.

In a funeral, the dopamine and attention related pathways may be highly activated and Jack may have sufficient stimulus to sit still. Taking behavior in a particular and unusual circumstance and using it to judge capability in another is at best unrealistic.

9. ADHD MEDICATIONS THE BASICS

Up to 70% or even 80% of people with ADHD who take medication and get therapy will have an amazing improvement. They may, for the first time *ever*, be able to enjoy studying, long conversations, or take care of the little details in their work.

The difference is so dramatic that Paul Wender, a major researcher who has treated hundreds of people with ADHD, roughly says "it can be more amazing than treating a depressed person with electroshock therapy."[12]

But there are risks to medication, especially side effects, and you absolutely first need to be diagnosed appropriately.

Once you reach that stage, you'll have to decide whether or not it makes sense to try a medication. To do so, you have to evaluate a lot of things. First, and most importantly, how significant are the symptoms? Are things in your life giving you trouble?

Even people with significant ADHD don't always need medication. I recently struck up a conversation with a casual acquaintance and mentioned I was writing a book on ADHD. He told me about a relative of his who, at age 8, was struggling in school and diagnosed with ADHD. With Ritalin, the kid has been a straight A student and is highly sought after by colleges.

Yet the kid stops taking medication during the summer, and does just fine then.

The fact is that people with ADHD have been around for as long as civilization has. We have more than our fair share of success stories. Having ADHD does *not* mean you're predestined to a bad life.

That said, as discussed, there are serious problems it can cause. The main three areas of trouble people with ADHD run into and that you may want to consider, are socially, professionally, and educationally.

Socially: are your friendships short, overly intense, or have unpleasant endings? Do you have difficulty developing long term relationships? Do you have difficulty staying with someone once you find them boring?

Professionally: do you often start projects and not complete them? Do you have difficulty finishing the small details? Is not taking care of certain things holding your career back, like not getting a promotion?

Educationally: do you have trouble sitting down and studying – despite being very motivated or strongly wanting to do so? Is your performance at school significantly lower than it should be considering your intelligence? Do you have trouble reading things from start to finish?

Other: do you have trouble listening, even when someone is talking directly to you? Do you go through many moods over the course of a day? Do you drive aggressively at times?

How can you analyze whether or not to take medications? A method I recommend is as follows. First, identify the strengths and potential problems of the options. Then determine what values are at play, and figure out the exact options.

Once you have all the relevant information down, you can use it to make a sound decision. Let's see how that works for the ADHD medication decision. The pros and cons are, of course, entirely personal, and you will have your own criteria.

Pros:

- If you have ADHD, medication can be life-changing. We're talking about the entire way you do things being better. Your ability to work on things will be improved, your ability to maintain healthy

relationships improved, you'll be more patient, and very likely more happy.
- In treating ADHD, most clinicians report that once a dose is reached – it can stay at that level for years and work just the same.
- You can stop taking medications at any time.

Cons:

- If you don't have ADHD, medication is a bad idea as it can be habit forming and have negative effects. That said, if you are experiencing those effects, you'll likely be able to stop quickly.
- If you take medication, you may become psychologically dependent on it. You might start to think things like, "I can't do it – I didn't take my Ritalin."
- You may be uncomfortable taking medication because you don't feel like you're different or abnormal and need it

- Medication might make you feel weird. (At the right dose ideally it wouldn't, of course.)

Values:

What values are at play? As follows are some that people with ADHD suggested:

- Wanting to be independent of medications.
- Wanting to be a good friend to my friends.
- Wanting to succeed in life, to perform well professionally. To succeed academically and be able to pass courses in college.
- Wanting to be able to do things that everyone else seems to be doing.

Finally, what options do you have? First, if you have ADHD, most likely you want to try some form of treatment. This is because, at the least, you have a different way of experiencing the world, and to get how the other 95% of the world works, you need help. That help could be a friend who really cares about you, a therapist, or medication.

- Try behavioral methods. About 30% people get results with this alone.

- Try alternative diets or exercise or other methods. Not such positive results but does work for some.

- Try medication. Up to 70% or even 80% of people get very significant benefit if done alongside with therapy.

If I do something on medication, doesn't that mean *I* didn't really do it?

You're not alone in worrying about this. Recently, I read this argument against using ADHD medications in a Presidential Council on Biomedical Ethics report.

A key component of learning, the ethicists argue, is making conscious choices to do something, and having to overcome the natural resistance. For them, taking an ADHD medication can undermine the value of all your actions, and teaches you nothing since when you stop, you're back where you were.[13]

This argument is on the surface very valid. But with my personal experience and based on all my research, strongly believe that it is based off an inaccurate understanding of the underlying condition, its severity, and progressive impact on self-esteem and ability to succeed.

It's common to think of people with ADHD as lazy. They might hear things like, "Why don't you choose to work? Sit down, study and do well!"

The problem is that people with ADHD are entirely capable of making the decision to sit down and *try* to study, just like anyone else. Unlike the typical person, however, after an extremely short period of time, they experience a strong sense of restlessness and lose the ability to stay focused.

This inherent difficulty focusing can be overcome. Doing so, however, is significantly harder than it is for someone without ADHD. At the right dose, medications for ADHD don't make the decision to, say, study that much easier – rather, they make it so that doing so for extended periods of time is not extremely difficult.

The moral decision is exactly the same. The only difference is in the ability to implement it.

Medication in fact makes the choice a meaningful one because it makes it possible to really choose between being productive and slacking off instead of choosing between *trying* to be productive (and failing) and not trying at all. As such, I find the President's Panel's argument to presume a capacity that simply does not exist.

That said, adults with ADHD do have responsibility. At the same time as they have a neurological disorder, if you don't make dinner, you won't eat. If you run a red light, you'll get a traffic ticket. And if you don't control your temper and push someone, you could very well go to jail.

It is an incredible challenge to manage the condition and gain meaning in life. Medication can make it possible.

This WILL Change How You Think About Medications

At the right dose, it's extremely likely that you won't notice the Ritalin, Adderall or Vyvanse working.

What?

To repeat, at the right dose, you hopefully won't feel the medication doing anything at all. This might feel very wrong –

after all, I bet the first time you took your med, you felt a complete difference. You actually were spending extended periods of times on things!

Initial treatment with stimulants often causes a slightly stronger effect than it will with time. The benefits aren't necessarily gone. Rather, the feeling of being in a different mental state might diminish.

To put it in other words, you might start an ADHD medication, several months later be really on top of things, responsible, and succeeding in many ways that used to be a problem. But if someone asked you if the ADHD medication was doing anything, you – *ideally!* – would say, "Not really."

If you want to check if it is working, you can come up with a list of symptoms and see how often they occur. ("Today, on a scale of 1-3, how much difficulty did I have paying attention to conversations?" And so on.) You may not remember well how you operated in the past which can make comparisons harder.

Make a list of the main ADHD symptoms. Be honest. Are they really the same problems they were at the beginning?

You might not still be convinced, but the following might help.

Take Joe Shmoe, a 45 year old with ADHD. Every day, he wakes up and has a strong cup of coffee – if he doesn't, the day just doesn't get off on the right note.

One day, diabolical researchers come in and change his cup of caffeinated coffee for boring decaf. What do you think happens?

It's pretty much impossible for Joe to notice the difference. He'll think that he had his caffeine fix and act like he did – but he'll perform worse than usual. All this without any conscious realization that there was no caffeine and that he is actually not at his usual work standards.

So if you think your ADHD medication isn't working, try this. Ask someone who you spend a lot of time with (and who isn't ADHD herself!) what she thinks. Or try, carefully of course, asking your boss if your performance has changed. You might be surprised at their reactions.

Paul Wender, who is, as mentioned, a major figure in ADHD research and someone who has treated many patients, argues that the following situation is actually fairly common. A couple, which had been going through some hard times, came to the realization that the husband may have ADHD, and he started treatment with Ritalin. Several weeks later, the couple came in for a follow-up.

When asked, the husband said that things weren't that different. His wife cut him off. "Are you crazy? Now I actually really enjoy spending time with you! You're a completely different person!"

I know several people who themselves don't believe that the ADHD medication does anything. When someone else is asked, however, they say that it has a clear difference.

The best person to judge how well an ADHD medication is working for *you* is someone who

lives/spends a lot of time with you, and doesn't have ADHD.

10. 10 QUESTIONS ABOUT ADHD MEDICATIONS

1) **What are the current ADHD medications?**

The most commonly used ADHD medications are the stimulants, which include Ritalin, Adderall and Vyvanse. The stimulants are quite effective and can make a tremendous difference for the better.

After the stimulants, as of writing, there are a two non-stimulant medications specifically approved for ADHD, Strattera and Intuniv, both of which seem to be effective but not as much as the stimulants, while potentially having less –

or different – side effects. Finally, there are a variety of other medications that seem to help with ADHD symptoms, but are not specifically approved for treating it, like Wellbutrin, the Tricylcic antidepressants, and Provigil.

See later in this book for a quick guide to almost all the commonly used ADHD medications.

2) What do the medications do and why do they work?

Stimulants work on your body to activate the sympathetic system. They increase your heart rate slightly and promote greater energy and focus. Specifically, they tend to work on the dopamine and norepinephrine chemical systems.

What they basically do is tell your body that something important is happening. This can help increase your focus, motivation and attention. While called stimulants, people with ADHD typically find them relaxing – it's like their brains are slowed down and can finally focus on what is in front of them.

The non-stimulants also activate attention related pathways, but do so by different ways.

3) Will taking Ritalin or Adderall will fix my ADHD/ADD and make my life that much better?

At the right dose, medication makes it so that you're a lot more like normal. But since when is everyone that happy?

Remember, when you start taking stimulant medications, you're changing how you experience the world. Some people compare the stimulants to like putting on glasses – you suddenly see the world like most people do.

That is true. But imagine that you now start seeing a whole variety of signals and things that you never before dealt with. You might, for instance, notice that a guy you thought was just being friendly is actually quite heavily hitting on you. And you're not sure of what to do.

Or you might realize that other people in your family may also have ADHD, and some of their habits start to irritate you – which is made worse because you know you have done the same things.

Even with medication treatment, you need to take care of yourself, develop solid work patterns and develop organizational skills. You might for the first time in your life realize how useful those things are.

For most people, it takes a good, understanding therapist to realize what's changing in their life and how to make sure it keeps going in a positive path.

4) Does Tolerance to ADHD Medications Happen?

Yes, absolutely. That said, all the clinicians I've encountered who describe their collective experience treating thousands of patients say that developing tolerance is somewhat rare.[12, 14, 15, 18]

Now, initial doses very often need to be adjusted. We want to use as little of the meds as possible because we can never forget how powerful they are – so start at the lowest dose. But typically, when a therapeutic dose is reached, it can stay they for years.

While this is generally true, a good idea may be to take occasional "drug holidays," or periods without medications. Maybe don't take your meds over the weekends when you're busy having fun, or every couple months take a week off.

But while there is a great deal of clinical experience that's positive, I have not read many (if any!) research papers specifically examining if tolerance to ADHD medications occurs over time.

Remember the previous point, however. It is entirely possible that your ADHD medication is doing its job – knocking your symptoms right into remission – and you still feel sometimes frustrated with your concentration, focus and so on. But that's entirely normal!

5) What's a sign that the dose is too high?

At the right dose, an ADHD medication should *not* significantly reduce your creativity, ability to enjoy things, or make you engage in mindless and overfocused work. If you take an ADHD medication and spend 3 hours washing an already clean floor – that's a **bad** thing and a sign of a too high dose!

The thing is, ADHD medications *won't* or shouldn't make you study, be a better listener, or whatever. What they should do is make it so that you're capable of choosing to do so. When you study, you'll react to the material. When you have a conversation and want to do so, your mind will stay on the topic and hopefully enjoy it.

6) Can you describe what it's like to take a stimulant?

The following stories both start the same exact way. An 18 year old freshman in college has just come to the library to get some studying done.

Version A: Not medicated, normal ADHD

Looks at watch. Okay, it's 3pm, time to study some chemistry. Soo boring!

Pulls out books, starts reading, taking notes. This is so boring. Darn, it's just so hard. *Looks at paper, blankly.* Didn't I just read that paragraph?

Rereads paragraph, tries to take some notes on it. Notices two people who just walked by and that they're talking about the College band. This is driving me crazy! The text is just so dense – who writes this stuff?

Tries again to read the first few pages.

Version B: Medicated ADHD

Looks at watch. Okay, it's 3pm, time to study some chemistry. Soo boring!

Pulls out books, start reading, taking notes. This is so boring. Darn, it's just so hard. *Look at clock* – only 5 minutes? Is the Ritalin doing anything? Okay, I just have to focus. Now what are the main classes of chemical bond? *Starts drawing a neat flowchart that summarizes the material quickly but thoroughly.*

Looks at watch. 30 minutes have passed.

30 minutes? That went by so fast! And I don't feel like ripping the book into pieces, running out the library, and doing something completely different!

7) How do you find the right dose?

There are different ways to find the right dose, but the safest is to start at the lowest possible and go up from there until the right amount is found. Other methods include starting at a higher dose and going down, but this exposes you to the risk of unwanted – and unneeded – side effects.

8) What are the risks of medication?

Stimulant medications can cause anxiety, suppress your appetite, and insomnia. Additionally, they may, at first, cause feelings of excessive confidence or pleasure.

Rarely, but not as rarely as we thought, they can cause psychiatric responses, like triggering mood swings or even psychosis – possibly in a normal person at a normal dose. Additionally, they may have cardiac effects, and so their use in people with heart conditions should be done carefully it at all.

For a full list of side effects, see the manufacturers insert. While overwhelming, make sure to weigh the risks against the benefits, and please note that these side effects usually go away once medication is discontinued if they are that serious.

Non-stimulant medications also have their share of side effects. Strattera may cause suicidal thinking, Intuniv may cause sleepiness and possibly fainting, and so on.

9) What if my friend wants to take my medication?

Your friend may have an important project to do and thinks that your medication might help, or may just be interested in giving it a try. But remember several things.

First, if you share your medication, you are violating Federal law in the United States, and are acting as a drug dealer. This is made even worse if you accept money for your medication.

Second, you have no idea of what other medications your friend is on, and what their general health is. If they suffer any significant side effects, you will be liable, and could be sued. Worse – you will be personally responsible, and will have let them down as a friend. A doctor has many years of education plus experience to make medication decisions as well as insurance to protect him if he makes a mistake.

Third, your doctor trusted you when she prescribed the medication to use it as directed. While relatively common, the decision to prescribe stimulants is monitored by the government. By sharing it, you are violating her trust and putting her at risk.

Finally, by sharing your medication, you are undermining the legitimacy of your using it.

10) What happens if I take an ADHD medication and don't have ADHD?

We used to believe that stimulants had a paradoxical effect in people with ADHD. That people without it who took them became over energetic and excited, while people with ADHD became calmer. As such, many doctors believe that a positive response to stimulant treatment is a good sign of ADHD.

Unfortunately, stimulants can also have a positive effect in people without ADHD. They are commonly used, for instance, by college students to cram the night before an important test. This is unfortunate, because it delegitimizes the tremendous benefit that they can have for people with ADHD.

For people with ADHD, medication can allow normal experiences to be possible. For someone without, and at high enough doses for people with ADHD, it can allow abnormal experiences.

11. 10 WAYS TO PROVE ADHD EXISTS

1) The brain wave qEEG test

qEEG brain wave scans have shown that people with ADHD have different brain waves. And those brain wave differences aren't just a theoretical construct that you can look at in textbooks. In a recent study, a mix of 500 people with ADHD and without were tested with qEEGs. The results?

It could tell with about 90% accuracy whether someone had ADHD or not.[16] Just by looking at the brain wave patterns. This is a clear sign that if you have ADHD, you are hard wired to think different.

2) People with ADHD have different sized brains with different behavior.

Imaging studies of people with ADHD have shown that their brains are smaller in certain places than people who don't have it, among other differences.[17] While this has not yet translated into a test that can accurately diagnose ADHD, it is yet another sign that there is an underlying physical cause of ADHD.

Additionally, some studies have shown that the brains of people with ADHD use energy in a different way.

3) **ADHD is transmitted according to genetic pattern**.

If both parents have ADHD, then their kid has a greater than 50% chance of also having it. The very high rate of heritance of ADHD occurs even if the kid is adopted and raised in a different house. This is crucial because it shows that ADHD is transmitted by genes.

If two babies are identical twins, that is, they have the same DNA, and one has ADHD, then other has a greater than 50% chance of also having it. If the two twins are not identical, that is they were born together but have different DNA, and one has ADHD, the chance that the other twin has ADHD is about 30%.

This means that messages contained in DNA cause ADHD. And if you get your DNA from someone who has ADHD, then you're also very likely to have ADHD.

The transmission of ADHD is not 100% determined by genetics because almost nothing in life is. Not even height, eye color or skin color.

4) **We can point to specific genetic mutations**

We're starting to be able to say that the D4R and other genes are associated with ADHD. It still isn't definitive – we haven't found a single gene that causes it, and probably won't. As a complex, neurological condition, ADHD is most likely caused by many factors.

Some mutations we're finding of particularly interest include those in the dopamine transporter and dopamine receptor genes. Not only do those mutations appear to be associated with ADHD, they are in the exact area expected – the dopamine pathways.

5) **Physical conditions cause ADHD symptoms.**

ADHD used to be called "Minimal Brain Dysfunction" because similar behavioral and attention problems were noticed in people who had suffered brain damage, like from a concussion or infection.

The vast majority of people who have ADHD don't have it because of head injury. But since brain trauma or damage has been shown to cause similar symptoms, it reminds us that neurological factors beyond our control are at work. For instance, damage to the frontal lobe can cause behavioral disinhibition.

6) **The symptoms of ADHD are *not* just extremes of normal behavior.**

There are more than 91 areas where people with ADHD are significantly more impaired than people without it. And the difference is downright striking. 0% of people without

ADHD in one study had trouble doing things in the proper order or sequence, while almost half of those with ADHD *did*.[3]

There are, of course, areas where they symptoms of ADHD overlap with normalcy. For instance, 19 percent of a control group experienced "easily distracted by irrelevant thoughts when I must concentrate on something." This is contrasted to 84% of people with ADHD.[3]

And there is a huge difference in the occurrence, persistence, and impact of the symptoms. Something with ADHD might only be able to focus on something challenging for *5 minutes* before being overcome by a sense of horrid, anxious boredom. This is a tremendous difference from the average person.

Now yes, any one of the symptoms can be argued to be an extreme of normal behavior. It is their sum, their persistence, and their highly disruptive nature that point to a clear difference.

7) **ADHD has been around for a long time**.

We only developed diagnostic methods for ADHD in the past century because until recently it wasn't as serious a problem.[8] If Fred in 1700 couldn't sit through class, that was OK. Fred could go work as a blacksmith. Nowadays, however, our society requires many years of paying attention and following prescribed social roles.

For people with differences in attention – the current system is brutal.

Also, the DSM diagnostic criteria for ADHD say that symptoms need to have started before age 7. For most of human history, simply surviving to age 7 was an accomplishment, let alone doing so and studying arithmetic, reading and getting along with other kids.

There are many historical figures who may have had ADHD. Benjamin Franklin, for instance, held dozens of jobs in his life. When he wasn't rashly flying a kite in a lightning storm, he was convincing the King of France to support America, or something entirely different. And in his many courtships, he inevitably got bored and needed to move on to something different.

All of which are associated with ADHD.

Other figures that may have had ADHD include favorites like Thomas Edison, Mozart, and possibly Einstein.

8) **People with ADHD have extreme behaviors**

Using a list of just 9 questions focused on behaviors, noted researcher Dr. Barkley reports being able to catch ADHD in an amazingly high percentage of cases. Just answering 9 questions can pretty much tell you if you have ADHD or don't.

If ADHD were nothing more than normal behaviors, just a little more extreme, this would *not* be the case. There would not be such a definitive difference between people who have it and don't.

The tests for ADHD detect people who have ADHD, and detect people who don't. This is because they look at areas that are very challenging for people with ADHD and that people without it hardly think about twice.

9) **Medications have an amazing impact**

People who have ADHD and take medication for it report an amazing difference. For the first time in their lives, they can sit through lectures, read books, and actually enjoy studying or having long conversations.

The impact of medication takes people who have struggled with so many things their whole lives and suddenly makes it possible for them to understand how other people function and behave.

Dr. Wender says that the difference between someone with ADHD and takes medications can be more impressive than the difference between a very depressed person before and after electroshock therapy! (We're talking about a guy who goes from lying in bed not eating to possibly dancing for joy).

The impact of treatment on people who have ADHD is incredibly striking. That it has such a difference, that the difference typically lasts as long as treatment does, strongly argues that the difficulties the person was having were due to a neurochemical difference.

10) **There is a solid model that explains why ADHD exists**

For ADHD to be considered a valid theory, it likely needs a strong reason for existing. After all, it seems like the symptoms it causes are bad things – and would be selected against by evolution.

People who, for instance, impulsively ate a new berry would possibly be poisoned and die. Or they might not handle their crops properly and starve, charge at a fortified enemy position, and so on.

There is, however, a strong evolutionary argument that explains both why ADHD exists and why it is present at the level it is.

The theory is that at first, in the early days of humanity, the characteristics associated with ADHD provided an evolutionary benefit. They could be great hunters, for instance.

With time, however, as society shifted towards a farming model, those benefits became disadvantages. That said, however, people with ADHD may be more likely to procreate at a younger age.

That, and the fact that they are often trailblazers, entrepreneurs, explains why they became rare but not nonexistent. 5%, or 1/20, is a significant amount, after all.

12. THE 4 SECRETS TO SUCCESS WITH ADULT ADHD

Here are the 4 things you must know if you want to succeed despite having ADHD.

1) If you have ADHD, you're different. Your brain works differently. You can't do anything about it directly (as far as I know, there isn't a brain exchange program - yet), and, whether you like it or not, it has a major impact on your life. *Most people aren't like you.*

There's a reason you've been having all the issues you've been having – it's not your fault.

2) **There are amazing things** about you that you don't appreciate. Other people simply aren't as energetic, friendly, interested in biofuels or spontaneous as you.

By focusing on your strengths, you will achieve great success and the respect, admiration and even envy of other people ("why can't I start my own art agency/legal practice?" and, "why can't I get that promotion?")

3) **Life will make it** near *impossible* for you to focus on your strengths.

You will instead focus on the fact that you can't sit still. That you have trouble having "normal" conversations about small, boring things. That you drive really fast, blasting music. Whatever the symptoms the ADHD causes – those are the things that will hurt and depress you.

And when you focus on the bad things, other people will too. People instinctively look to other people for social guidance, how to judge things, even more so than you might think. (People with ADHD can be quite resistant to group think because they can't ignore that nasty voice inside of them saying, "this is stupid!")

If you are down and unhappy about your flaws, other people will see and judge them the same way you do. They'll think, "wow, that guy's not normal."

If you focus all your energy on doing things that you feel you have to, but are excruciatingly hard, you'll never be happy. And you won't do them that well anyways!

Your gift is in certain areas, certain things, certain strengths. You are AMAZING at those things but don't realize it. And trying to do the things you can't, that people without ADHD can do easily, is a sure fire way to fail and be unhappy.

Would you expect a great and passionate painter to spend his time filling tax forms? Or the CEO of the company to mop the floor?

The Hunter/Farmer model proposed by Hartmann is very empowering and just makes sense to a lot of people. As we've discussed, it argues that people with ADHD are more like hunters – they need constant stimulation, variety, excitement and change.

Other people are like farmers – focused, able to do boring things for long times, and conventional.

Now, remember, ADHD isn't just a matter of feeling, or personality types, or lifestyle. (Although based on how many executives I know have ADHD, it can actually be an advantage at some jobs). It's a neurological condition that we have pretty much proven is a physical condition.

If you have ADHD, your brain has different wave patterns and activity than people without it. Your basic energy processing system is different, as well as the way that you respond to stimulation. For you to maintain focus on something, it has to be very, very interesting.

We're starting to be able to prove that by pointing at specific brain activity and abnormalities.

4) **If you have ADHD, you are still fully responsible for your life**. But treatment can change

everything. That's not just hyperbole. We're talking about a complete change in everything – for the better. Even so, and even though ADHD is a real problem that can make your life *hell* at times, you're still responsible for everything you do.

If you have ADHD and you run a traffic light – you still get a ticket. If you don't do your homework and miss the final, you'll get an F.

Remember, most other people are simply too busy to care about whether or not you have ADHD. They care about what you do, whether they enjoy spending time with you, doing business, or whatever. You are the only one ultimately responsible for your life.

And, ADHD or not – how can you make it a great one?

13. DR. TUCKMAN ANSWERS QUESTIONS ABOUT ADULT ADHD

Dr. Ari Tuckman is the author of "More Attention, Less Deficit: Success Strategies for Adults with ADHD" and "Integrative Treatment for Adult ADHD: A Practical, Easy-to-Use Guide for Clinicians".

He has treated hundreds, if not thousands, of adults with ADHD. He generously took the time to answer questions that readers of mine have submitted over time.

What attracted you to ADHD?

I actually fell into it around 1998/99. I was starting out and was approached about working with some patients who were adults and had ADHD. They needed help dealing with their condition and with life management. I took the opportunity and it was a good fit.

At that point, things were different. If you knew three things about ADHD – than you were an expert on it. It's better now, but still not good enough.

What kind of experience do you have with adult ADHD?

I've been focused on that area for 10 years now and a significant percentage of my clients have ADHD. If I had to put a number, I'd say I've treated hundreds if not thousands of patients with adult ADHD.

Why do we not know enough about Adult ADHD?

The problem is that doctors, especially primary care physicians, aren't good at recognizing it. And even if they are, they're not in a good position to do something about it because they simply don't have the time for a thorough evaluation, which can take a couple hours.

Very often people have ADHD and their doctor just doesn't notice. It's tough for the doctor, of course, because clinicians have to know a million things. But when it's your life, you expect them to get things right.

Why is this a problem?

Very often a doctor will notice that someone with ADHD has anxiety or depression and treats only that. They are then surprised when there isn't such a good response and think "I guess this person just doesn't respond well to treatment."

And it's unfortunate. Untreated ADHD is a big set-up for a lot of problems. We have hundreds of studies that show the kind of bad impact it has on your life.

Can you elaborate on the problems ADHD causes?

It's a big misconception that having ADHD is no big deal. It has severe consequences on people's lives. ADHD has measurable effects in all areas of functioning. Everything is affected by it – social life, work performance and more. Its effects can even go as far as your credit rating!

ADHD has the most impact of almost all psychiatric diagnoses because it is always present and always causing problems.

If you could tell a Doctor two things about ADHD, what would they be?

First, that even if someone was hyper as a kid, they don't have to be hyper now to have ADHD. And they might not be restless or overactive in your office.

Second, that having ADHD doesn't mean you're not successful. On the contrary, there are some really successful people who have it. But it comes at a great cost and they have to work harder to achieve their success.

Remember, I'm a psychologist. That means that I prefer talking to people. But for ADHD, I am a big fan of medication because it works. And it works well. Proper use of medication sets people up for success so that other strategies will be more successful.

Medications for ADHD like Ritalin and Adderall have their fair share of controversy. What's your opinion on that?

I'm certainly not advocating that everyone has ADHD or should take ADHD medications. Everything stems from a proper diagnosis. Once that's done, choosing to use an ADHD medication is a lot like choosing to use painkillers. You do it if you need to, and otherwise don't. I had surgery, for instance, and for a short time, needed to use strong painkillers.

It's not a matter of good or bad, but rather how medication fits into your overall treatment plan. Medications for ADHD tend to be very effective.

What are your thoughts on the proper use of medications like Ritalin and Adderall?

First, I'll repeat that it's absolutely essential that a proper diagnosis be made before using any medication. I have a saying that accurate diagnosis guides effective treatment.

It's also important to have realistic expectations. You can take a pound of medication and still not do any work. The fact is, you still have to choose to put in the effort. Medication puts you in the ballpark, but you still have to swing the bat.

How do you choose a medication?

Typically, I recommend an extended release. That means either Adderall XR, Concerta, Vyvanse, or Focalin XR.

To choose between them, I find the rule of thirds to be quite useful. Roughly one third of patients will respond best to Adderall or Vyvanse, one third to Ritalin/Concerta/Focalin, and one third will respond equally to both.

You can't point at a hundred people and say that for everyone Adderall or Ritalin would work best, but for any one person there may be a better or worse response.

For my patients, it can be hard, but they have to realize that it can take some time to figure out the right dose. It's not a magic pill, and you have to be somewhat lucky to get the right dose on the first try.

Doctors sometimes are too cautious and might use a child-sized dose in an adult. Then they're surprised when they don't get good results. That's like wondering why half an aspirin doesn't help an adult with a headache. It doesn't mean that a larger dose wouldn't be more effective–up to a point, obviously.

What are some issues you see in treating adults?

Adults who are diagnosed or deal with ADHD are different from kids because they've been dealing with their situation undiagnosed for most of their lives.

They've had to come up with explanations for why things are not going so well in their lives. And they've constantly been telling themselves, "Now it's going to be different. I'm going to get that report in on time, listen more when people talk, spend my money better, etc."

They've had a lot of failures.

For a kid, there aren't those years and years of struggle.

Most adults when diagnosed have a tremendous sense of relief. It puts things in place. And it's an explanation that isn't pejorative or judges them badly.

They've probably heard way too many times things like, "you're irresponsible," or, "you're lazy." A diagnosis of ADHD is much better than that.

How do you diagnose ADHD?

I typically do a 2 hour interview. If possible, I have a parent or romantic partner come along to give additional input. I try to get as much data as possible, including old report cards which can be particularly telling. Of course doing so is often hard in someone over 25.

We look at how the person is doing now and at prior points across a broad range of situations. Looking at just one area can be misleading – how are they performing overall? And does ADHD fit the pattern of data?

How would you respond to critics of diagnosing ADHD?

For most psychiatric – and even a lot of medical – diagnoses you look at symptoms and history. Blood tests can't tell you everything. The best diagnosis, of course, has to be thorough. If you do a good job, you'll look for the right things while not asking leading questions.

Some symptoms are more obviously associated with ADHD. What are some of the more unusual or harder to notice things?

A lot of people with ADHD have difficulty retaining what they've read, and may not actually read books that often. Magazines and websites are easier to digest. It's common to have to reread things.

Other areas include careless mistakes in math. They know how to do something, but mess up on the small details. Everyone has brain glitches like that but they are more common in people with ADHD.

A really interesting phenomenon I see is that sometimes people with ADHD will have done homework assignments but forget to hand them in. This is particularly telling because there isn't an alternative explanation. If someone doesn't do their homework, for instance, you could say that they just don't want to do it. Blame it on motivation. But there's really no reason you'd choose not to hand in an assignment that you did.

Another area is losing things, both in the house and out in the world. There's really no advantage to losing your cell phone, for instance, so doing so is an indication that ADHD may be an issue.

Some psychoanalysts might say losing your phone is a sign of subconscious conflict?

That just doesn't seem very likely. Remember, that psychoanalytically based treatments have not been shown to work that well for treating ADHD. That's not to say it can't help with other issues that folks with ADHD or other people might have, but it won't change the underlying condition.

Some research has shown that low levels of iron in the blood has been associated with ADHD. What do you have to say to that, or claims that bad diet causes ADHD?

I've heard things like that often. Parts of those claims may be true, but you have to remember that correlation does not mean causation. While it is true that men in general are taller than women in general, being tall, for instance, doesn't make you a man.

A possible explanation, however, could be that people with ADHD may not have as healthy diets. It's important to remember, however, that dietary treatments have not been shown to a valid treatment for ADHD.

How do you decide to use a medication or not?

It's a question of weighing the demands of things going on in your life against your abilities to manage them without medication. What other strategies, for instance, could you useto handle your life? If the demands of your life outweigh your ability to handle them, that's an indication that medication might help.

Of course, if someone shows up in my office, they're probably not doing as well as they would like!

And of course there are different situations. You may need to take medication during the week but not so much over the weekend.

One of the biggest fears people have is that their ADHD medication will stop working. In your experience, does tolerance to, say, Ritalin or Adderall develop?

Not usually. It is my experience that, once you find the right dose, you can keep taking it for years, even on a daily basis.

That said, there are some factors that may change the right dose. Sometimes there is significant weight change which can change how effective a dose is.

Also, someone may find that their lives require them to perform at a higher level when they might get a promotion with more responsibility and really have to be on their game. Or when they have a new baby.

What are some thoughts you have on ADHD in general?

Getting diagnosed with ADHD can be really life changing. Suddenly things make sense. I have to tell my clients that I understand how hard things have been in the past. But now they're in a new situation.

With medication, things can be quite different. And, although they've already heard a million suggestions, in therapy we look at new strategies that are based on a solid understanding of how people with ADHD tend to process information, so we can create strategies that are more likely to be helpful.

Anything else?

Today I'm having a client who is living out of the country and coming back home here in America to visit his family. He's driving four and a half hours here and another four and a half hours back, a total of nine hours driving, just so we can spend two hours to officially diagnose him with ADHD.

14. YOUR CAREER AND ADHD

How do you find what is the right job for you if you have ADD/ADHD? It can be challenge, especially if you are demoralized. You may have spent so long in your life doing things and failing at them or simply not succeeding – that you simply don't believe in yourself that much anymore.

The good news? With treatment, it is highly likely that things will change for the better.

That said, there are jobs that are good for people with ADHD and jobs that aren't ideal matches. For instance, being a TV show host might be perfect for someone with ADHD, while being a tax auditor could become overwhelming with the sheer amount of details and "boring" work.

The key to your success is simple. You need to identify the areas that you find interesting and perform well in, while accepting that your condition will make some things hard for you.

What do you spend your free time doing?

_____

_____

_____

_____

_____

_____

_____

What is something that, when you do, hours can pass by without you noticing?

_____

_____

_____

_____

If you met someone, what topic of conversation would keep you talking for a long time?

_____

_____

_____

_____

_____

_____

Those three questions are aimed to help you realize that there are areas you naturally excel in/find interesting. Don't feel bad if you wrote down something that isn't necessarily a great job attribute ("love playing video games").

It may just indicate that you need a job that, and this is crucial, *has a similar reward structure*! Why do video games hold your attention so well? Because they push your attention buttons, rewarding your engagement quickly and providing feedback. Now all you need is a job that does something similar and it will go by just like that!

What are three things you want to accomplish in your life? Forget thinking about what you can't do – if you *could* do anything, what would those things be?

1) _____
   _____

2) _____
   _____

3) _____
   _____

Is there something on there that you wish you could do but personally believe you can't?

For instance, getting an advanced college degree or getting a promotion at work – both are common goals (for everyone!) that people with ADHD can have a lot of trouble with. The key is to realize that a) your ADHD has been preventing you from succeeding b) if you treat it or find ways to neutralize it, you *will* succeed.

Here are some jobs that can be prefect fits for people with ADHD.

Jobs that involve Crises:

1) *Emergency room surgeon*. Don't believe it? Imagine that you're in the hospital, chatting with a friend when the following happens. A kid is wheeled into the ER room, screaming.

Everyone is clearing a path to let the emergency team bring him in. A nurse hands you surgical tools. "You have to operate now, Doctor, or he's going to die." What do you do?

People with ADHD don't have as much of a focus problem when it is a clear crises. They may actually switch into a super focused mode where they are both extremely calm, able to focus on the work, and do a great job.

2) *Diagnosis specialist.* Let's say Mr. Ahmed has been suffering from a strange cough, weird spots on his toes, and dizziness – but only when he brushes his teeth. Either he's completely crazy, or suffering from a rare condition. His family calls you, desperate for help. What do you do?

This isn't obviously exciting as the first, but medical specialties that require creativity, thinking outside the box, and a connection with the patients – those can be great jobs for people with ADHD.

4) *Crisis PR Specialist.* Company X is being attacked all over the

television and radio stations because of a stupid comment that one of their employees made after having one too many drinks.

They're at risk of losing **millions of dollars** worth of respect and brand loyalty from its customers. It needs someone to figure out how to handle the crises and resolve it. They actually are a good company, and the employee did in no way represent their views, but if they don't handle the situation right – it could be a disaster.

Your phone rings. "Hey, please. We need your help, right now." What do you do?

5) *Lawyer.* Your client, Mr. Smith, is being wrongfully accused of violating some laws.

The jury pool is angry because the crime he is accused of is heinous, but you spoke with him and you know one thing - he's innocent.

The only way to get him off is to say the right words so that the jury will view the case against him the way that they should – as an absurdity. But the lawyer for the prosecution is a grilled veteran who will instantly respond to any steps you take over the line with an objection.

The evidence is quite compelling against your client. It would take a feat of oratory and persuasion to save him. What do you do?

Jobs that involve change:

6) *Head of technology.* You spend your day doing what you want, walking around,

keeping up with employees. Your official responsibilities include making sure that the company has the latest technology and is using it well.

Because you're a high level position, you have secretarial support for all the small details, and you can focus on keeping up to date with the latest, coolest things in technology – while being able to do something else when you get bored.

Your boss wants some things from you, but since you pretty much tell him what he wants from you, the job is a breeze. Because you stay abreast of all the new things easily, this job is fun for you.

15. THE 10 MOST IMPORTANT ADHD MEDS EXPLAINED

If your doctor prescribes you a medication for ADHD, likely it'll be on this list. Reading this should quickly inform you as to what you need to know.

With any medication, you have to balance the benefits against the risks.

The ADHD medications are powerful and can make a tremendous difference for the good in those that take them and have ADHD.

That said, they can also have significant side effects.

Note: There are some variants including Focalin that are variants of the medications on this list but are not given their own entry.

#1) **Ritalin**

Extremely popular – almost a synonym for ADHD – Ritalin has been a star since it was made in the 1940s and named after a chemist's love, "Rita."

Ritalin's technical name is methylphenidate.

Ritalin acts on dopamine and norepinephrine, to block reuptake from the space in between cells. This increases the amount of time they stay there, which means that they activate signaling pathways for longer periods of time.

And that means greater focus, motivation and attention.

With therapy, up to 70% of people with ADHD experience significant benefit from Ritalin. The effects can be amazing, allowing normal living for some – to repeat, it is a powerful medication that can make normal living possible for some people.

One of the biggest downsides to instant release Ritalin – and all the stimulants – is that the benefits only last a matter of hours, from 3-6. This can mean you have to take several doses a day, which can be inconvenient.

That said, there are longer release forms which provide symptom relief for much longer periods of times, as long as 12 hours or such.

While the most effective treatment for ADHD, stimulants like Ritalin have their fair share of side effects, however, including anxiety, weight loss, and potentially even psychiatric issues like triggering mania or psychosis. Additionally, they can cause heart problems in at risk people.

Because Ritalin has a high potential for addiction and abuse, it has the highest restriction possible while still being widely used – it's a Schedule II drug.

Pros: With Adderall, Vyvanse and so on, the most effective chemical treatment for ADHD

Cons: Potentially serious side effects, schedule II, figuring out dose schedule can be a pain

Variants: Concerta, Focalin, Metadate, Daytrana

#2) **Adderall**

Adderall has become extremely popular for treating ADHD since its introduction in 1996. It is a mix of several amphetamine salts and like Ritalin is a highly effective treatment.

Some studies have shown that Adderall may be slightly more effective than Ritalin at treating some of the ADHD symptoms. This advantage is not established, but probably has to do with a slightly different mechanism of action. One dose of instant release Adderall, however, may last as long as two doses of instant release Ritalin.

Adderall may also have a slightly different side effect profile than Ritalin.

In terms of chemical action - Adderall not only blocks the reuptake of dopamine and norepinephrine through cellular pumps, it also goes inside the cells and reverses the pumps. So instead of letting those chemicals in, and taking them away from "outside" the cells, it kicks them out.

Reversing the pumps may theoretically lead to the build up of free radicals, but no major study has analyzed whether this happens or has a clinical impact.

Adderall has the same downsides as Ritalin, and is also schedule II.

Pros: Among most effective treatment for ADHD

Cons: Potentially serious side effects, schedule II, figuring out dose schedule can be a pain

Variants: Adderall XR

#3) **Vyvanse**

Vyvanse is an extended release form of Dexedrine that has gained a reputation for being a smooth medication which is more easily tolerated than many others. This is due to its release mechanism that is linked to slow digestion.

Vyvanse fundamentally is nothing more than Dexedrine, which has been around for a long time and developed a bad reputation due to its over-use as a diet pill.

That said, there is something quite good about Vyvanse/Dexedrine – it's made only from the d-type of amphetamine with none of the the l-type. Which is great because it's quite possible that the d-type is more effective and/or has less of the side effects of the l-type.

Adderall, by contrast, is a mixture of d and l-amphetamines, which means that it more may have more of a kick as well as more or different side effects. This mix may mean that Adderall may provide more of a "punch" so to speak.

That said, Vyvanse has its fair share of side effects.

The good things about Vyvanse include its quite long lasting effect, possibly up to 14 hours, and its somewhat less susceptibility to abuse. It is as effective as Adderall and Ritalin for treating ADHD.

Pros: Among most effective treatment for ADHD

Cons: Potentially serious side effects, schedule II, dosing can be a pain

#4) **Intuniv**

Intuniv is a treatment that was initially used for lowering blood pressure and has only recently become more fashionable for ADHD, which recently resulted in its approval for treating ADHD. It's pretty much the opposite of the stimulants, which raise blood pressure and stimulate the body.

Why might Intuniv work for ADHD then? Well, its exact biochemical mechanism of action is unclear, but it seems to work as an alpha-2 agonist.

These receptors are regulatory, but may also serve to activate – so to speak – certain areas of the brain, meaning better focus and attention.

Intuniv is like a stronger Strattera, but hopefully avoids the problems of the stimulants, and may even be useful in combination with them. There are problems, of course. One of the trials which led to its approval had a shockingly high rate of people fainting – something like 5/262 participants fainted.

That is not a good side effect. Additionally, treatment with Intuniv just falls short of sending ADHD into "remission."

Other issues possibly include depression and blood pressure problems.

Pros: Non-stimulant, may be moderately effective

Cons: Possibly serious side effects like fainting, less effective than stimulants. Very new and untested.

Variants: Clonidine, Guanfacine, Intuniv

#5) **Strattera**

Strattera used to be "the only non-stimulant treatment approved for ADHD" until Intuniv came onto the market in 2009.

Like Ritalin, Strattera also works on the norepinephrine chemical and prevents its removal from the space in between cells. Despite a similar mechanism of action, it does not have work immediately, however. It can take up to 8 weeks for Strattera to show its full benefit.

Strattera is supposed to provide all day coverage taken just once, but one study showed that taking a dose in the morning and at night provides the best release. This is still a significant advantage over the stimulants.

The history of Strattera is somewhat interesting - it was initially tested for use in depression, but didn't seem to do much. Researchers thought that its effects on norepinephrine might have benefit in treating ADHD, and they were right.

Similar to the antidepressants, Strattera does increase your risk of becoming suicidal, which is why it has a black box warning.

The studies show that Strattera works, some say even as well as Ritalin. But those claims to efficacy seem somewhat overstated, with many people saying that Strattera is not so effective.

Strattera is worth a try when stimulants fail or are not a good idea (say you have serious anxiety or past psychosis), yet it also has some of their nasty side effects.

Pros: "Non"-stimulant, long term coverage

Cons: Suicidal ideation, may not be as effective, expensive, long time to take effect

#6) **Provigil or Modafanil**

There's quite a buzz around Provigil, generic modafanil. It keeps enough of the amphetamine like behavior of Adderall to provide the kick needed to treat ADHD, while having a host of other chemical behaviors that, some argue, may make it less addictive and less risky.

Provigil, for instance, is only schedule IV, as opposed to the highest restriction placed on Ritalin and Adderall.

That said, we don't know a lot about it. Provigil may play with the dopamine receptor like Ritalin – or it might not. It might just increase levels of dopamine by some other mechanism. This is important because the way it interacts with dopamine may determine its potential for addiction.

Other chemical behaviors of this drug? Hold your breath – it possibly has GABA, serotonin, adrenergic, histaminergic and glutamanergic effects. That's like half of the neuro-transmitters currently in vogue, and some of them theoretically cancel each other out!

(While there are hundreds of neurotransmitters, because of how little we know, we basically pretend there are only about 10. Hopefully, as we learn more, we will get even more effective treatments with fewer side effects.)

Provigil is used, in part, for sleep apnea, narcolepsy and has been proposed for schizophrenia, which is stunning, considering that traditional stimulants cause psychosis, not treat it.

As of now, however, Provigil is not approved for treating ADHD, although it seems to have decent efficacy in treating it. (Some studies have shown similar efficacy to Ritalin, one – from the manufacturer itself (!) – showed no efficacy, and so on). A major study trying to approve it for ADHD in children failed when a significant amount of children developed skin rashes.

So we don't know how well it works. And Provigil is also extremely expensive, so playing around with it can rack up a bill.

Expect interesting things from this drug and its half-dozen chemical actions.

Pros: May be less addictive, may be as effective as stimulants, schedule IV

Cons: Expensive, new, not-approved for ADHD, not enough long-term use data

#7) **Wellbutrin**

Wellbutrin is a strangely behaving antidepressant. It's an alternative treatment for ADHD, although not approved for that use like Strattera, and has been shown to be better than placebo for treating ADHD.

That said, Wellbutrin has only a modest benefit for ADHD, with some studies showing that it works to some degree and others showing that it doesn't really work that well.

What Wellbutrin does is act as an inhibitor of reuptake of norepinephrine and dopamine – to some degree. It also mimics them somewhat, which is interesting. Chemically, Wellbutrin is eventually converted by the body into some form of amphetamine, which might explain why it has some impact for ADHD.

So it isn't the best treatment for ADHD, but it is used not-rarely.

Side effects can include extreme anxiety. We're talking potentially about really bad anxiety. That said, in addition to making you less depressed, Wellbutrin might just help you stop smoking – which is another of its uses.

Pros: Moderately effective, full day coverage

Cons: Extreme anxiety as a potential side effect, not as effective as stimulants, turns into amphetamines eventually – so may have similar problems

#8) **The Tricyclic Antidepressants (TCA)**

The tricylcic class of antidepressants has been shown to have significant benefit in treating ADHD, although not as strong as the stimulants. They are not so often used because of their serious potential for cardiac toxicity among other side effects.

The TCA's benefit for ADHD is separate from their potential antidepressant effect. This is highlighted by the fact that reduction of some ADHD symptoms, especially behavioral, may start occurring in less than a week, as opposed to the 3-4 weeks it takes for the antidepressant effect.

(It's an important distinction to make because you could feel like the King of Morroco but still have significant ADHD symptoms.)

They are many drugs in the TCA class. Of them, desipramine may be the best for ADHD, then imipramine.

That said, it is possible that other issues like antagonistic behavior may emerge with treatment,[12] meaning that you exchange one set of symptoms for another.

On the other hand, treatment with TCAs may provide almost full-time coverage. You don't need to take 5 doses a day, for instance, as may happen with some forms of Ritalin.

Note that newer antidepressants, especially the selective serotonin reuptake inhibitors like Prozac and Zoloft have not shown similar efficacy or benefits in treating ADHD. This may be due to their more specific behavior, and lack of effect on norepinephrine.

Pros: Modest efficacy, long term coverage

Cons: Heart toxicity, overdose possibility, possible new symptoms, not as effective as stimulants

#9) **Risperdal**

This medication is a very popular tranquilizing antipsychotic. It basically blocks dopamine receptors, reducing levels in the brain. Careful readers may wonder if, Risperdal lowers dopamine levels, how can it be a treatment for ADHD?

The answer? Because. Just because. It doesn't make 100% sense, but it's certainly happening, most likely based on word-of-mouth and publications that discuss it as a possibility. And Risperdal has been approved for treatment of agitation and aggression in autistic kids. Its sedative effects may make it attractive for treating kids who have ADHD and are a handful.

Just remember, long term use of Risperdal may lead to permanent movement disorders, extreme weight gain, and diabetes.

Pros: Sedating, may help fall asleep, may help gain weight

Cons: Long term side effects. Is pretty much the exact opposite of traditional ADHD treatment

Variants: Any anti-psychotic class tranquilizer

#10) **Exercise**

Exercise is, in its own way, for many an incredible help for ADHD. Within healthy moderation, it has no side effects (though people taking stimulants should be careful) and can honestly be said to be nature's cure for ADHD. It relaxes the mind and body, increases concentration, and improves mood.

One kid used to be a handle in school, but when his teachers agreed to let him run around the schoolyard when he got restless, did OK. That kid? Winston Churchill, one of the greatest British leaders ever.

Now, it's true that exercise is unlikely to provide true relief from ADHD symptoms. But it's also for sure not going to make you become psychotic, manic, stunt your growth, make you faint, give you diabetes or make you suicidal.

Please note that exercise has not been shown to have anything near the positive benefits and effect in treating ADHD symptoms that other medications have.

Other Drugs of Interest: Pemoline or Cylert – a schedule IV drug with moderate ADHD efficacy. Withdrawn in US from market due to toxicity to liver. Desoxyn – basically methamphetamine, not used often because it's "meth," which has very bad associations

16. 25 LIFE TIPS FOR ADULTS WITH ADHD

1) **Buy and use a planner**

One of the biggest challenges for people with ADHD is to stay organized and to get round to doing the small things. Once you get a planner and start scheduling things – and, this is the key part, actually doing them, your life will become that much easier.

Make sure you respect your planner. Don't put in it things that you won't get round to doing. Be realistic. Think of your planner as a way of promising yourself that you will do something. Empty promises dilute the value of your word.

2) **Exercise several times a week, rigorously**

For people with ADHD, exercise can do wonders. It can improve concentration, mood and attention while burning off some of that extra energy. And it makes you look better and feel better. Aerobic, high intensity workouts are the best.

If you get bored at the gym, try watching television or reading a book. Work your way up! You may not be able to do an hour long workout immediately, so do what you can and slowly improve.

3) **Promise little, do much**

People hold you to your promises. If you say something – then don't do it – you've lost credibility. You may find yourself especially likely to be over optimistic about things you're excited about. But when you always meet your word, and exceed it, people know they can trust you. And they associate you with excellence.

4) **Think "why am I here?" if you get bored**

Sometimes it's hard. You're with someone, and you're just not connecting, or you're at an event and you're just standing near the wall.

Why are you there? What do you want?

In all areas of life, being able to think bigger and gain perspective refocuses you and lets you achieve. When you get bored or frustrated, reminding yourself of why you are doing something can make it that much easier.

5) **Multitask to your advantage**

Some people with ADHD do best while multitasking. For instance, some may have their best conversations while walking or doing something with their hands, like chopping vegetables or playing a video game. Or some may pay better attention in a lecture or meeting if they doodle.

Don't be ashamed of your ability, or perhaps need, to multitask!

6) **Use visual reminders**

If you have to do something, put a big stick it note in a prominent place. Seeing it will probably help get you to start working. For instance, one student had to read several research papers but kept procrastinating.

Finally, he decided to simply leave a window on his computer open with them – within a few hours, he got so annoyed at having the window open that he just read the papers and got it over with.

7) **Listen to music**

Some people with ADHD focus best when they have background music playing. The theory goes that instead of getting distracted by something unexpected, the music "distracts" you, but you expect it to, so you stay on task.[17] Additionally, music may activate emotional regions of the brain and create greater stimulus, meaning better focus.

8) **Sleep at meetings**

I heard of a famous economist/mathematician who would always spend meetings with his eyes shut and leaned back. Anyone who didn't know him assumed that he was sleeping. At the end, he'd lean forward and ask the most penetrating and interesting questions.

He learned best with his eyes closed, and he wasn't worried what people thought about him. Neither should you feel bad about how your ADHD express itself.

9) **Think of your positive traits, not your bad ones**

A study asked one group of people to think of themselves as very smart and competent before taking a test. The other group in the study was told to think of themselves as inferior - stupid. Naturally, the positive thinking group scored significantly higher.

Before an important event in your life, stop. Focus on your positive traits.

10) **Commit yourself to your goals in a public setting**

If you want to do something, let people know. Make promises to the people who matter in your life. It'll keep you focused, on target. And being accountable makes you succeed.

11) **Drink tea or coffee**

For people with ADHD, tea and coffee can make great friends. Tea especially has health benefits. Of course, use moderation, and check with a doctor before mixing caffeine with stimulant medications.

12) **Do one thing**

Pick one habit you'd like to have, something small and easy. Now do it, always, without compromise or fail.

The power of succeeding at one thing has radical effects.

Once you get in the habit of holding yourself accountable, and doing things, you'll find it easier to face other challenges. The journey of a thousand miles begins with the first step.

12) **Call or email someone who you haven't seen or spoke to in a while**

Don't fall into obscurity! Reach out to your friends. Not only is socializing good for your health and fun, it increases creativity and gives you a deserved break.

13) **Present yourself professionally**

If you provide a service, have business cards. Have a website! People with ADHD can especially have difficulty realizing how accomplished they are, and putting in the effort to focus on your accomplishments and how to present them best can be both enjoyable and rewarding.

14) **Give, always give**

People naturally return favors. If you are nice to people, people will be nice to you. Of course, it goes without saying that sucking up and being nice just to gain favors is a bad idea. Be genuine.

15) **Cultivate a happy, positive attitude**

Having ADHD is not always fun, but your life should be enjoyable and meaningful. Think about the good things you have and train yourself to look at things positively. Because often the way you view something determines what it is or becomes.

16) **Deal with paperwork once**

The paperwork and small tasks can easily add up to an overwhelming mound. Make it a habit: *if you can deal with something immediately, do so.* If you can deal with an email right away, do so. This will improve your efficiency and reduce how much time you spend on annoying small tasks.

Note: Be careful not to send important emails impulsively without double-checking.

18) **Be eager to greet people, and do so with a smile**

19) **Humility**

Remember where you came from – a drop. Remember where you'll go – a grave where worms will eat you.

And remember what you'll leave behind – the memories of what you did.

20) **Listen**

Ask relevant questions, be interested, and listen. Extremely hard for anyone to do, especially for people with

ADHD, but well worth it.

21) **Learn from everyone**

Everyone has their place and their time. Everyone can teach you many interesting things that you didn't know or with a fresh perspective. Keeping that in mind will transform how you think of people.

22) **Have a great photo of yourself**

Having a photo of yourself that looks great will help you out in surprising ways. Online, for instance, having a great photo in your profile will improve the way people think of you. Most importantly, it might even help you think better of yourself.

23) Treasure your family

No one else loves you like they do. Always put your family first – they're among the only people who really deserve it.

24) Review your flaws

We all have negative traits that get us into trouble time and time again. People with ADHD especially have issues with organization and impulsiveness. The great philosopher Maimonides said that the best way to overcome a negative trait, is to do the exact opposite until doing so becomes second nature.

That might be a bit difficult for us normal people. But know what your flaws are – and, more importantly, do something to remedy them.

25) Treasure opportunities to stand out

When someone has a birthday, write them a meaningful card or send them a personal email.

Always be ready to make someone feel special. Did anyone ever do something that made you feel wonderful? Now go and find a way to do that for someone else!

17. 10 STUDY TIPS FOR PEOPLE WITH ADHD

Succeeding academically can be especially challenging if you have ADHD. Here are 10 study tips that will make your life that much easier. Because they aren't all about studying, it's worth looking over even if you aren't in college.

1) **Buy a scheduler/planner** if you don't have one already. Do it today – it's that important because everything stems from preparation. And once you get one, use it! Each day, make it a habit to plan out your activities for the day.

At the same time as you need to learn how to schedule your time – and, this is the most important part, actually do what you schedule – you absolutely must respect your capabilities.

A quick way to burn out is to try too hard, and setting goals you can't meet ensures that you'll fail.

Don't say you'll spend 2 hours studying when, honestly, all you can do is half an hour.

Make reasonable goals. Be flexible. If you didn't get 1 hour of math done at 12 but got 30 minutes at 11 and 30 minutes at 1, that's just as good.

2) **Make eye contact with the teacher**. Of course, you shouldn't be staring at them, but a little eye contact helps you focus, subtly shifts their attention to include you more, and is a solid way to keep attention high during a long lecture.

3) **Sit in the front of the room**

4) **Schedule your homework**.

If you have a large math problem set, make yourself start doing it as early as possible. If the set is due on Thursday, it might make sense that, starting Sunday, you spend one hour each day on it.

Now, once you've scheduled your homework, you absolutely have to do it. Missing a day is not a good idea. It's procrastination and that is a sure fire way to get into icky situations that make you unhappy.

If you push off the math homework to Wednesday, you'll have a crappy, stressful day then – and you probably won't finish the problems. Not only that, the worst part is that even if you do all the work in one marathon 4 hour session (or perhaps 2 hour, assuming you can get some panicked hyper-focus magic going), you won't learn nearly as well as if you had spread the work out.

Advance planning. Working towards set goals, one step at a time. Amazing success.

5) **Reward yourself**! If you just aced a difficult midterm, then buy that shirt you wanted, get a beer with a friend (if you're over 21) or just dig into a pizza with extra cheese.

Once you start setting goals and meeting them, you'll have something to be proud of. The things you buy or do for yourself as a reward for succeeding mean *a lot*.

6) **Tackle the hard stuff first**. Research shows that if we make doing fun things rely on doing not-so-fun things, then we are much more likely to do the boring stuff. Additionally, sometimes it's best to tackle the challenging material when you have the most energy and strength.

7) **Take advantage of office hours**. Get to know the professor as a person, meet them, and actually discuss the material with them. They are an expert in the field and truly love the material, otherwise they wouldn't have become professors.

This will make the class that much more interesting. Be honest – would you rather learn from some stranger, or from someone you know, admire, and like? And it's a great way to build professional contacts as well because professors tend to be very well connected.

And there's more. Research shows that students who develop strong relationships with college faculty are much more likely to do well.

8) **Get the help and support you need**. If you have a diagnosis of ADHD, then, according to the American with Disabilities Act, you're entitled to certain accommodations like possibly extra time. But the college doesn't have to give them to you unless you give them plenty of notice and appropriate documentation.

Take care of that as soon as possible. As much as we've progressed in the last 20 years, many schools can still be quite resistant, and they love bureaucracy. You don't want a professor who doesn't believe in your condition to be able to mess up your education!

9) **Take smaller classes**. In a class where your professor will notice your absence – and care – you're much more likely to come. And going to class is the absolute number one

requirement for doing what you're supposed to be doing – learning. Smaller classes tend to be more informal, relaxed and exciting. Which is exactly what you want.

10) **Build yourself up**. This is the most important tip and especially important for people with ADHD. Even if you just started taking Ritalin or Adderall and feel like you can take on the world because you can finally concentrate, be careful.

It takes a lot of time to develop the ability to work for extended periods of time, to focus and work hard. People who don't have ADHD spend all of high school slowly improving their study skills and work ethic. It's not fair, but you're at a disadvantage to them. For now.

Change yourself for the better! Push yourself. But take it easy and make sure that you're not pushing too hard. If you're running a race, a sure-fire way to burn out is to start running hard at the beginning, burn out, and not be able to run even at a moderate pace for the rest.

Life's like that – one step at time, slow and steady, and always push yourself to do just a little more.

18. DISTINGUISHING ADHD FROM OTHER PSYCHIATRIC DIAGNOSES

It can be very hard to tell if a set of symptoms means ADHD or something else. On the one hand, up to 80% of people with ADHD will also have some other psychological condition.[3] On the other, conditions like depression and anxiety have symptoms that overlap with ADHD, and bipolar mood disorder extremely overlaps.

Depression: Up to half of people with ADHD will also suffer from significant depression at some point. This is because of all the challenges and difficulties that they will face. They will not be able to perform at the same level as their peers, and will naturally become unhappy.

The key point is that the depression is reactive. It is logical. If you have to hold down a job and get promoted to support your family, but you can't because you constantly forget to hand in paperwork, then it makes sense for you to get somewhat depressed.

This means that the depression may not be overwhelming or all consuming. A typical person with depression may want nothing more than to lay in bed. A person with ADHD and depression may have just as serious depression, but become temporarily cheered up when something good happens, say an invitation to a fun party.

This also means that it can be very hard to gauge depression in someone with ADHD because they often are simply too energetic and/or inattentive to appreciate their state.

Fortunately, often the depression will go away upon treatment for the main symptoms of ADHD. Once you are able to take care of the small details, get the promotion, your depression may also lift.

But if the depression is crippling in and of itself – the person doesn't feel good enough to try anymore and has become seriously despondent, then it may require taking care of first. That said, the treatments for depression and ADHD can overlap and take place at the same time.

Bipolar: People with ADHD are often confused for someone with bipolar and vice versa. When a person is manic, they think extremely rapidly without seeming connection, have a great deal of energy, and are impulsive. Those are all characteristics of ADHD as well. Check out the official DSM diagnostic criteria for ADHD and bipolar. They overlap at 2/3 of the criteria.

Distinguishing between the two needs to focus on mood. Someone with bipolar typically has mood patterns that last for extended periods of time. For a while, they'll be very energetic and happy, and for a while very sad.

It is an up-and-down pattern that takes some time. Additionally, people with bipolar may lose touch with reality all-together, and either become paranoid or have delusions of grandeur.

People with ADHD also have rapid mood swings. But they're almost always reactive and don't tend to last for more than a couple of hours. Additionally, someone with ADHD doesn't typically lose touch with reality.

There is a big caveat, however. People with ADHD may seem to observers to have lost touch with reality when excited about a new project.

"So I'm going to get my friend's lawyer to invest in this new start up idea I had a few days ago which is going to change how we do business in the coco bean manufacturing index; I just need to raise $100,000 which I can do..."

This is the kind of energetic speech that could come from someone who is manic and starting to develop delusions. It can also be from someone with ADHD who is honestly quite excited about the breakthrough coco bean manufacturing method he came up with while "finishing" the reports for a completely unrelated project at work.

Additionally, take the person with ADHD who just came up with his exciting new plan. He may stay up really late working on it because he simply can't stop thinking about it.

This is different from someone who has bipolar and stays up all night because they can't calm down. In the ADHD case, it's a matter of intellectual engagement and excitement, while in the bipolar it is a matter of mood and euphoria.

If the two sound similar, that's cause they are. An important difference may be that the person with ADHD who stays up late working on the project will probably feel tired the next day (even if he keeps plugging on!), while people with bipolar who miss sleep tend not to feel it.

Distinguishing between ADHD and bipolar becomes even harder when you realize that they can happen together. In that case, figuring out an appropriate treatment can be a real challenge, as stimulants for ADHD can trigger manias.

18. ABOUT THE AUTHOR

So who wrote this book?

My name is David Gurevich. I am a student at Brown University studying Business and Biotechnology. While not a doctor, I have studied biology for several years and have read hundreds of medical articles, written more than 170 articles myself, and published an article on stem cells.

My writings on ADHD, particularly medications, have been very popular online. Additionally, I was involved with a research lab at Harvard Medical.

Nothing in this guide is meant as medical advice, (I am in no way qualified to give it) but rather as my opinion supported by the sources I looked at.

What do you know about ADHD?

I have ADHD, but didn't really believe it existed or was causing me problems. Unfortunately, my performance in school was skydiving and my life a general mess. Since deciding to confront my condition and get treatment, I have become an expert in search engine issues, started a popular medical blog and am performing excellently in school despite taking courses that are quite challenging.

Heck, I even wrote this book.

Writing this book was hard. Time and time again, as I conducted the research, read the papers, interviewed people - I saw myself. This guide is what I wish I had several years ago; hopefully it will help readers avoid making the same mistakes I did.

If you have any questions or believe anything can be improved, please let me know at: dg_writing@hotmail.com

19. RECOMMENDED READING

Adult ADHD: What You Need to Know

1) ADHD in Adults: What the Science says, Russell A. Barkley, Kevin R. Murphy, Mariellen Fischer

This book was of immense help in writing this guide. It is definitely worth a read. The only downside is that it is written from a very scientific perspective, which may make it not as accessible as possible. That said, it is a sterling work.

2) Attention-Deficit Hyperactivity Disorder in Adults, Paul H. Wender

Dr. Wender's work was also of great help in writing this guide. Explores the phenomenon of ADHD in adults and explains many aspects about it.

3) Fidget to focus : outwit your boredom : sensory strategies for living with ADD / Roland Rotz and Sarah D. Wright

A book that explains strategies for overcoming ADHD issues like boredom. Worth reading if you want to figure out ways to live life better despite ADHD.

4) ADD success stories : a guide to fulfillment for families with attention deficit disorder: maps, guidebooks, and travelogues for hunters in this farmer's world / Thom Hartmann ; foreword John J. Ratey, MD

Another very useful book that explains how to live life successfully - despite having ADHD.

20. SOURCES

1) Recognizing ADHD in Adults with Comorbid Mood Disorders: Goodman DW, Thase ME.

2) The Complexity of ADHD: Diagnosis and Treatment of the Adult Patient With Comorbidities, Newcorn JH, Weiss M, Stein MA.

3) ADHD in Adults: What the Science says, Russell A. Barkley, Kevin R. Murphy, Mariellen Fischer

4) Epileptiform abnormalities and quantitative EEG in children with attention-deficit / hyperactivity disorder, Fonseca LC, Tedrus GM, Moraes C, Vicente Machado A, Almeida MP, Oliveira DO.

5) DSM-IV Criteria for ADHD

6) ADHD in College Students: Developmental Findings, Weyandt LL, Dupaul GJ.

7) Attention-Deficit/Hyperactivity Disorder in Adults: Recognition and Diagnosis of this Often-Overlooked Condition, Feifel D, MacDonald K.

8) ADD success stories : a guide to fulfillment for families with attention deficit disorder: maps, guidebooks, and travelogues for hunters in this farmer's world / Thom Hartmann ; foreword John J. Ratey, MD

9) Nutritional and Environmental Approaches to Preventing and Treating Autism and Attention Deficit Hyperactivity Disorder (ADHD): A Review, Curtis LT, Patel K.

10) Nutrition in the Treatment of Attention-Deficit Hyperactivity Disorder: A Neglected but Important Aspect, Schnoll R, Burshteyn D, Cea-Aravena J

11) Identifying the neurobiology of altered reinforcement sensitivity in ADHD: A review and research agenda, Luman M, Tripp G, Scheres A

12) Attention-Deficit Hyperactivity Disorder in Adults, Paul H. Wender

13) Beyond therapy : biotechnology and the pursuit of happiness / a report of the President's Council on Bioethics ; foreword by Leon R. Kass

14) Answers to distraction / Edward M. Hallowell and John J. Ratey

15) Long-Term Tolerability and Effectiveness of Once-Daily Mixed Amphetamine Salts (Adderall XR) in Children With ADHD, McGough JJ, Biederman J, Wigal SB, Lopez FA, McCracken JT, Spencer T, Zhang Y, Tulloch SJ

16) The Clinical Role of Computerized EEG in the Evaluation and Treatment of Learning and Attention Disorders in Children and Adolescents, Chabot RJ, di Michele F, Prichep L, John ER

17) Fidget to focus : outwit your boredom : sensory strategies for living with ADD / Roland Rotz and Sarah D. Wright.

18) Phone and email discussion with Dr. Ari Tuckerman, Vice President of the Attention Deficit Disorder Association.

CPSIA information can be obtained
at www.ICGtesting.com
Printed in the USA
BVOW09s1108280417
482622BV00001B/8/P